government policy in this area. This book must be read by anyone keenly involved in international trade."

TAKESHI KONDO
Senior Vice President
C. Itoh & Company

"Americans are becoming aware of the complexities, problems, and benefits of an increasingly trade-dominated, competitive, interdependent world economy. Few know as much about one growing aspect—countertrade. How this technique functions in decisions on purchases of military equipment, fertilizer factories, telephone systems, and much else, is the subject of Mr. Schaffer's fascinating book, which suggests that Americans need to become shrewder traders as well as more efficient manufacturers."

HAROLD BROWN
The Johns Hopkins Foreign Policy Institute

"Following the debt crisis, a growing number of countries needing America's goods and services are unable to borrow freely traded currencies necessary to purchase these commodities. It is encumbent upon those interested in increasing our exports and decreasing the related trade deficit to apply the necessary talent and energy to reach those markets. Countertrade provides an essential response to this dilemma and Schaffer's book is an intelligent and useful guide to this important activity."

WILLIAM LOUIS-DREYFUS
President
Louis Dreyfus Corporation

WINNING THE
COUNTERTRADE WAR

WINNING THE COUNTERTRADE WAR

New Export Strategies for America

MATT SCHAFFER

WILEY

John Wiley & Sons

NEW YORK • CHICHESTER • BRISBANE • TORONTO • SINGAPORE

Schaffer, Matt.
    Winning the countertrade war: new export strategies for America / by
Matt Schaffer.
        p.   cm.
    Bibliography: p.
    ISBN 0-471-63252-X
        1. Countertrade—Case studies.   2. Countertrade—United States.
    I. Title.
    HF1414.3.S32 1989
    382—dc19   88-18683
                                                                                CIP

Printed in the United States of America

10 9 8 7 6 5 4 3 2 1

For Christine Cooper

Contents

Contents

Contents

Acknowledgments

This book began in a discussion with Jim Stein, my agent at William Morris. Without Jim's advice and encouragement it could not have been written.

A major aim of this book is to provide as a public service information about a collection of countertrade techniques and opportunities that are too little understood in the United States. I have gone to great lengths to accommodate the sensitivities of people who very graciously agreed to be interviewed. In several instances, I was allowed to use the information, but asked not to identify the informant. My occasional use of terms such as "a company" or "an official" complies with these requests for anonymity. In the rare cases where I was asked not to include material, it has been faithfully excluded.

I believe that all the material in this book is publicly available, although not easily accessible. All the transactions involved at least two parties, a buyer and a seller (often a trading company was one of the parties), and were usually known to both the U.S. commercial attaché in a country and the attaché's foreign counterpart in the United States.

Acknowledgments

Several of the transactions have been reported in the press or discussed at countertrade conferences. My principal sources for the transactions presented here were, at various times, all of the above.

I would like to thank the following corporate officials who have been especially helpful: Cary Viktor of General Dynamics; Michael Cosgrove, vice president of Countertrade and Barter at the General Electric Trading Company; Pat Hall, vice president and director, Rockwell International; Chuck Martin, director of licensing and countertrade at Westinghouse; Dan West, director of Monsanto's countertrade operations and chairman of the American Countertrade Association; Rich Buttleman, vice president of Caterpillar World Trading; Patrick Hanafee, vice president of Motors Trading (General Motors); George Horton, executive vice president of MG Services; Philip Rowberg, vice president for countertrade at Douglas Aircraft; Francis Hamilton of the International Finance Corporation; and Murray Scureman, vice president of Amdahl Corporation. Valuable assistance was also provided by Jim Hill, director of procurement at Raytheon; Thomas Snyder, president of N-Ren International; Don Hart, a lawyer with Guilfoil, Petzall and Shoemake in St. Louis; Milton Brown, senior trader with CMS Trading of Washington, D.C.; Don Oglesby, chairman of Peak Technologies in Scottsdale, Arizona; Jim Barkus, a New York countertrade consultant; and François Boucly, a Paris-based countertrade lawyer. Several U.S. officials contributed insights or material that proved to be of great value. They include Hal Ponder, an attaché with the U.S. embassy in Madrid; Pompeliu Verzariu, the U.S. Commerce Department countertrade specialist; and Robert Shipley, U.S. Commercial Consul at our embassy in Mexico City. Among the foreign officials I would like to thank are Werner Kaelin, the Swiss Defense attaché; General Ernest

Acknowledgments

Tomasso, the Dutch Defense attaché; Gabriel Wujek, the Polish Commercial Consul in New York; and Endre Juhasz, the Hungarian Commercial attaché in Washington.

Several friends and former business colleagues, while not contributing directly to this study, have greatly enhanced my general understanding of the countertrade issue, especially the following: Dr. Harold Brown, Secretary of Defense under President Carter; Stuart Eizenstat, managing director of Powell, Goldstein's Washington law office; Jody Powell, chairman of Ogilvy and Mather Public Affairs; Frank Carlucci, Secretary of Defense under President Reagan; the investment banker, Rod Hills; John Moore, president of Bechtel Development Corporation; Curt Hessler, senior vice president of Unisys; Takeshi Kondo, senior vice president of C. Itoh and Company; Grant Green, Assistant Secretary of Defense for Manpower and Reserve Affairs; Jennifer Stockman, president of Stockman Associates; and numerous members of the Export-Import Bank of the United States.

Many thanks are due to Johnnie Prather for her editorial assistance and to Sheila Taylor and Marjorie Banks for their help with typing the manuscript.

Writing this book, of course, would have been impossible without the gentle kindness and supportive understanding of my wife Christine and my sons Grayson and Ethan.

MATT SCHAFFER

Bethesda, Maryland
January 1989

A Struggle
for the Light of Day

Every book has obstacles that must be overcome before finding its way into print. This book has had its share. As a businessman working in the field of countertrade, I certainly have greater access to transactions than does a journalist or scholar. Indeed, many of my friends and colleagues in countertrade gladly contributed to this book. However a few, for perfectly valid reasons, were unable to share information. A comment on this may help to put into perspective dilemmas presented by countertrade.

In one business meeting I attended a few years ago, I heard the president of a large foreign trading company recount in detail the basic concepts of a remarkable countertrade transaction. In the early stages of this book, I wrote to him to say that the transaction seemed to be a classic example of how countertrade can fulfill a corporate strategy when the simple, direct sale of a product for cash will not work. I asked his permission to use the example in the book and requested more information about the transaction.

Like countertrade itself, his reply was indirect. He sent a copy of my letter back to my former employer, threatening both of us with legal action if I revealed anything about the transaction. In understandably stern and ominous terms, the employer wrote to deliver this message. I got the message.

Believe me, this transaction does not appear in this book! Shaken by this harrowing episode, I repressed the details and cannot even fully remember the transaction. I seriously began to wonder: if countertrade made people this jumpy, perhaps the book should be abandoned.

Countertrade is certainly not illegal, but it often depends on exceptions and on creative trading. Many companies regard at least certain aspects of countertrade, such as pricing, in a proprietary way. They correctly feel that using countertrade techniques gives them a strategic advantage. They do not want a competitor to learn how to structure a countertrade transaction, or how to use it in the resolution of trading barriers in a country.

A countertrade executive with a U.S. company summed up very well this dilemma of sharing information: "I don't want to tell about all the bad deals we chased that did not work out. That would make me look stupid. I don't want to tell you about the ones that did work because none of our competitors is working in the country. They might learn how to compete with us there. Most of all, I don't want to do anything to encourage the increase of countertrade in our field. Unlike the defense industry, we don't have much countertrade." He graciously agreed to talk with me but grew increasingly nervous with each draft of one chapter, no matter how I tried to accommodate him. First, he wanted his name removed, then the name of his company, and finally all reference to its countertrade activities. The good material he initially gave me had been restructured into verbal pablum. I was forced to totally rework the chapter and to find information for it from other sources.

There were other more conceptual difficulties in writing this book. My training as an anthropologist gives me a natural interest in the deepest levels of structure and in underlying principles. For these reasons, a chapter on tribal barter is included. Two reviewers commissioned by the publisher had widely divergent views on the chapter. One thought it contributed nothing of use to business people and thought it should be removed. The other thought it offered unique insights into the business of countertrade and said it was the best chapter in the book.

The first reviewer also thought that my desire to influence government policy on countertrade hopelessly tainted the book, that I should have confined this work to an analysis of countertrade itself.

I find it difficult to talk about countertrade outside the context of government policy. Congress has only recently begun to consider the subject in a series of hearings. Suspicious of what U.S. companies are doing in the field of countertrade, some members of Congress are already talking about passing new restrictions. The negativism of many U.S. government agencies is an attitude I would like to see changed. Whether we like it or not, Congress and the executive branch are beginning to scrutinize countertrade closely. American businesspeople will be affected by any policy on countertrade that emerges, even if Congress acts only to ask multilateral negotiators to control requests for countertrade and offsets. We cannot escape the linkages of countertrade and public policy in the United States.

WINNING THE COUNTERTRADE WAR

Chapter One

Countertrade Basics

*"I don't want to tell our competitors
about how we used countertrade to
make a breakthrough in a country."*
—Corporate Officer, Major U.S. Exporter

Most of the substantial U.S. exporters are absolutely inundated with requests for countertrade from countries around the world. Yet the practice is still poorly understood in the United States. A major objective of this book is thus to explain to the general American public what countertrade is, how it is done, and why countries feel they need it so badly. A practice that is literally sweeping through the world of international business needs to be brought forward and debated and understood by the public.

Most of what has been written about countertrade overwhelms the reader with definitions and technical complexity. I will try to avoid this pitfall by using examples and describing the fundamental structure of countertrade rather than an array of functionalist classifications.

Anyone who wants to understand missiles learns a basic principle: for every action there is an equal and opposite reaction. The principle can be applied to countertrade. In every international countertrade transaction, no matter what the shape, there is product flowing in one direction, representing a sale. The sale creates the need for a separate stream of products and services, often flowing in the opposite direction and always linked to the initial sale.

When General Electric (GE) needed to sell a turbine generator to Rumania and loan financing fell through, GE accepted Rumanian products as payment. When Rockwell desperately needed a way to win a printing press sale in Zimbabwe, the successful sweetener was Rockwell's offer to export ferrochrome and nickel from Zimbabwe. When General Dynamics (GD) needed to sell F-16s to Turkey, they offered to build a whole aircraft industry there and to invest in hotels and other projects as well. When McDonnell-Douglas needed to sell commercial aircraft to the People's Republic of China, they offered to build a plant there, to assemble the planes and to manufacture some of their components, all within the People's Republic..

Transactions such as these are what *countertrade* is. The term refers to all these types of transactions, to all forms of linked trading. There are numerous countertrade terms but the following four are essential to understanding.

BARTER

The Rumanian transaction with GE, described above, is *barter*. Rumanian products were traded out over time as a substitute for money, once the financing fell through. GE got paid only when it sold the Rumanian products it accepted through its trading company. The French countertrade lawyer, Jean-François Boucly (of Debost, Falque, Carpentier and Barbé), told me that in the dozens of countertrade contracts he has drafted, he has never seen one barter successfully put together. "They are by far the most difficult to structure. Countertrade always fares better if there is some kind of financing mixed in with the barter." Chapter 8 gives considerable detail about a remarkable commercial barter transaction carried out by N-Ren International, in which commercial bank letters of credit played a helpful role.

COUNTERPURCHASE

The Zimbabwe–Rockwell sale is *counterpurchase*. Zimbabwe paid cash through financing to buy the printing press. Rockwell agreed to compensate for Zimbabwe's expenditure by purchasing (actually *counterpurchasing*) ferrochrome and nickel from that country and exporting them. Rockwell earned a profit in the usual manner from the sale part of the transaction, and hoped to get all or most of its counter-purchase money back when it sold the Zimbabwe minerals on the world markets.

Counterpurchase is frequently used in Yugoslavia and Eastern Europe, where formal counterpurchase is necessary for most importing. This allows Magmedia in Yugoslavia, as discussed in Chapter 11, to sell computer disks to U.S. companies needing counterpurchase credit in order to sell their own exports to Yugoslavia. The value of the imports generally cannot exceed the value of the exports. A similar counterpurchase system has been adopted at a formal gov-ernment level by many South American countries struggling to balance their overall imports and exports, to stabilize their currencies, and to reduce inflationary pressure. Some compa-nies develop the exporting themselves when confronted with such counterpurchase requirements. Curragh, an Australian mining company that is a partially owned subsidiary of the U.S. oil company Arco, often pays a modest commission to a German trading company, Ruckhauser, to facilitate a sale of coal into Eastern Europe. The foreign exchange generated from Ruckhauser's trading is available to pay for Curragh's coal imports.

OFFSET

The transaction involving General Dynamics and Turkey is an *offset*, a package of transactions carried out over a specific time to compensate a country for the loss of cur-rency, jobs, and local technology development. *Offsets* are often required in large military purchases. Under the offset, the sellers—GD in this instance—must bear the cost of "direct" *offsets*, that is exports, services, or investment di-rectly related to the sale. GD must also pay for "indirect" *offsets*, which are general exports, services, or investment not directly related to the F-16 sale. As discussed in the next chapter, GD plans to fulfill much of the Turkish offset with investment for its own account, and relies very little on outside trading companies. In contrast, Raytheon pursues an effective procurement policy to deal with its smaller offset obligations, purchasing components from countries where it has offset obligations.

CO-PRODUCTION

The transaction involving McDonnell-Douglas in China is built around a *co-production* scheme. The buyer and seller in this case will collaborate to build an aircraft assembly factory in China. The co-production scheme will transfer technology to the new Chinese factory, not only to facilitate the assembly of planes, but to aid in the manufacture of some components for the plane. There is often a co-production component in a large military *offset*, as is true for GD in Turkey. However, co-production is so important to the concept of countertrade that it is often the major objective of a foreign country's request for countertrade.

ORIGIN OF COUNTERTRADE AND BARTER

How did this countertrade system of business first get started? In a general sense, forms of countertrade and barter have been around presumably since prehistoric times and all throughout history whenever money was scarce. Chapter 13 analyzes some tribal concepts of barter in a search for similarities with corporate barter. The tribal version has some important differences when compared to its corporate counterpart but does emphasize the extreme importance of the concept of reciprocity, which is an almost structural component of human nature and society.

Gabriel Wujek, the Polish commercial attaché in New York, has traced modern barter and countertrade through Eastern Europe back to Germany after World Wars I and II. Money was scarce in Germany after the wars because of extensive devastation. The practice arose naturally in this environment and was picked up by Eastern Europe, through geographic ties to Germany, in order to deal with its own nonconvertible currency (the government of Yugoslavia, for example, does not allow dinars to be freely exchanged for a "hard" currency such as dollars or yen).[1] Outside of Eastern Europe, a surge of recent countertrade dates from the succession of oil price increases in the 1970s. I have focused on this most recent cycle of countertrade.

UNITED STATES GOVERNMENT POLICY

This book also discusses countertrade in the context of current United States government policy, which is for the most part still negative and not very supportive, even though many U.S. companies and most countries of the world are actively engaged in it. For the record, here is a statement summarizing the United States government's position in a paper prepared by the Office of Management and Budget (OMB) (see Ref. 2, p. 11).

> The U.S. Government generally views countertrade, including barter, as contrary to an open, free trading system and, in the long run, not in the interest of the U.S. business community. However, as a matter of policy, the U.S. Government will not oppose U.S.

companies' participation in countertrade arrangements unless such action could have a negative impact on national security.

I believe that countertrade is not so harmful; if done well it can even be helpful to U.S. companies in many ways. U.S. policy on countertrade should be changed.

This book is not a catalogue of all major countertrade transactions and does not pretend to be comprehensive in this sense, nor is it a historical text documenting the evolution of countertrade. The U.S. Department of Commerce has been building a data base on commercial, nondefense barter transactions, and OMB[2] has at least begun the difficult task of recording a comprehensive list of defense offset transactions undertaken by U.S. defense contractors. The willingness of U.S. defense contractors to disclose information voluntarily was impressive.

Let me emphasize that countertrade is a secretive and therefore a very difficult subject to write about. Companies are understandably reluctant to talk about pending transactions or even old ones, if revealing a certain approach or key trading company would cause them to lose a competitive advantage, especially against foreign bidders. One corporate official who provided me with excellent information was very candid on this point: "I don't want to tell my competitors about how we used countertrade to make a breakthrough in a country. On the other hand, I don't want to talk about how we tried a countertrade deal and botched it up."

Most corporate officials view their countertrade triumphs with justifiable pride. The transactions involve considerable creativity and unbelievable diligence, sometimes taking years to complete, and they wish to share their experiences so that others may learn how to do countertrade well or will at least recognize the countertrader's unique achievements. To facilitate dialogue within a U.S. business community, the major U.S. defense contractors who export recently formed the Defense Industry Offset Association (DIOA). Even within this collegial group there is fundamental disagreement over how widely information should be disclosed; certain members are reluctant to share information with their fellow members, for fear of having their business positions eroded. A similar countertrade association, the American Countertrade Association, has been formed for commercial, nondefense transactions.

SUBCONTRACTORS

In general, U.S. companies are being forced to cooperate with one another increasingly to enhance their competitive positions. One ironic benefit of military offsets, especially, is that they facilitate and practically oblige cooperation. In satisfying an offset obligation, the prime contractor often requires its subcontractors to contribute. Offset credit is now given if exports and investments in a country by an unrelated third party company can be tied to the initial offset (i.e., GD gets offset credit in Turkey for an automotive investment that Rockwell made there). Increasingly, companies are using their extensive networks to find out in advance about such third-party investments, to get offset credit for them. The result is corporate cooperation. In barter and counterpurchase, alliances are also required with trading companies to sell off goods obtained in these transactions.

The usefulness of networks, alliances, and subcontractors means that the larger companies clearly have an advantage in putting countertrade sales together. They have more sourcing (purchasing) capability and can shift purchasing around the world to meet countertrade requirements. They have more capital for investment schemes and a richer variety of technologies to choose from in transferring technology under an offset requirement. Of course, their size gives them more leverage in negotiating favorable countertrade arrangements with a country and in requiring subcontractors to participate. In this very real sense, the rise of countertrade has given new meaning to the now old and successful concept of the multinational company. The large company with numerous subsidiaries and contacts overseas is in a good position to offer countertrade packages based on sourcing (purchasing) and co-investment or co-production. At least the "multiconnected" large company is in the best opening position to plan its countertrade moves, provided it has skillful players.

On the other hand, the smaller company is more at the mercy of its prime contractor, both generally and when it comes to offsets. Eileen White presented some interesting arguments about this issue in a front-page article in *The Wall Street Journal*.[3] She argued that subcontractors are more vulnerable and suffer more from foreign offset requirements than prime contractors. She cited the example of Menasco Texas (a subsidiary of Colt Industries), a landing gear maker that supplies General Dynamics (GD). When GD won an F-16 sale to NATO, Menasco was obliged to transfer technology to the DAF company in the Netherlands and now faces DAF competition around the world. The same Menasco scenario repeated itself when GD sold F-16s to Japan.

Another U.S. company with a similar problem felt unable to disclose any information because it might jeopardize its subcontract with the prime contractor. The vulnerability of subcontractors is a difficult problem to solve because their major goal has to be winning and keeping new contracts. This is also the natural priority of the prime contractor confronted with a request for offset and technology transfer as well. The potential ability of a prime contractor to bully subcontractors by extracting favorable offset commitments must be balanced with a hard reality. Without an attractive overall offset package the pime contractor does not win the sale either. Companies must be free to work out this complex issue relating prime- and subcontractors among themselves.

CORRECT APPROACH

As Congress and the White House become more aware of countertrade, I hope they will continue to resist the temptation to strive for more legislation restricting the flexibility of U.S. companies in this area. This is the wrong approach and focus. Many U.S. companies have become very good at countertrading. This has helped them overcome other U.S. disadvantages, such as interest rates higher than those of Japan, West Germany, Switzerland, and certain other exporters and our comparative lack of sufficient government export financing. The correct focus of Congress and the Administration should be on the governments of Europe, Canada, Australia, Japan, and other nations who require offsets officially for military and certain other purchases.

I believe two approaches toward foreign governments will work to control the rapid spread of military offsets. One is to negotiate directly through the GATT (General Agreement on Tariffs and Trade) talks in Europe for control in various areas of countertrade such as defense or telecommunications. A second, bolder approach is to develop selectively an offset policy of our own, requiring certain major exporting companies to the United States to take more responsibility for exporting from the United States, as is done in reverse by *all* of our trading partners in military sales, one of the few areas where the United States enjoys a trade surplus. Our valuable trade surplus in the military area will be subject to increased foreign pressure, generated through their requests for offsets, if we take no action as a government and if we fail to develop our own countertrade policy.

I proposed these two ideas to a group of some forty U.S. commercial attachés brought together for a Georgetown University symposium from our embassies around the world. They appeared to like the GATT approach because it stressed diplomacy. There were mixed feelings about various facets of a U.S. offset policy. Some of the officers reacted favorably to having the Pentagon continue to purchase military products from overseas, while insisting that the selling companies be required to export from the United States under U.S. offset guidelines that could be established. Outside the military area the officers expressed concern about applying the policy generally to countries with huge U.S. trade surpluses such as Japan, West Germany, Taiwan, and South Korea. A few officers believed that even a serious debate about such a policy could at least be a valuable bargaining chip.

The basic problem of military offsets for U.S. companies is that they are at the mercy of foreign governments and are no match for them. U.S. companies are practically obliged to comply with a foreign government's publicly stated policy in the countertrade area. It is often the law of the host country. The United States government could improve the U.S. company's ability to cope with offsets by interacting through diplomacy and by promoting the prospect of offset measures of out own.

If the United States government moves to regulate military offsets domestically, there is a danger that new rules might be applied to countertrade generally, including barter, counterpurchase, investment, technology transfer, and other approaches outside the military area. Commerce Department export licenses, if applied stringently, are already sufficient to deal with the valid issue of preventing technology transfer under an offset that might damage national security.

It is easy to rush to judgment and to assume that military offsets, which favor overseas sourcing (purchasing) and technology transfer, automatically cause jobs to be exported from the United States. The issue is more complex. A December 1985 OMB paper concluded just the opposite, claiming that the fulfillment of offsets actually created jobs in the United States because many sales would have been lost without attractive offset packages.[2] I am not trying to argue that offsets are necessarily good, but the culprits are foreign governments rather than U.S. companies struggling to export.

My perspective is that of a businessman who has also served in government and could not have written the book without the valuable insights of business colleagues and friends. Another source of information was a round of interviews conducted with numerous foreign commercial attachés based in Washington. My overall impression is that foreign countries skillfully and aggressively use government to advance their trade positions, whereas our outmoded *laissez-faire* approach has contributed to a steady erosion of our trade position.

No single measure, such as allowing the dollar to fall, will cure the U.S. trade deficit disaster. It will take a combination of tactics. Business, of course, must work on price, efficiency, and quality and include countertrade in the development of sales strategy. But government must also play a role with financing where necessary and with a supportive appreciation of the many benefits of countertrade as a technique and as a policy.

Chapter Two

Framework: On the Fringes of Export Credit

"Please tell your Pentagon that unless they offer the U.S. suppliers a U.S. government credit or guarantee, we are going to pull all of you from the frigate sale. We already have German and Italian suppliers and government financing lined up to replace you."
—Official of a European Shipbuilding Firm

OBJECTIVES

This book seeks to accomplish three major objectives. First, countertrade is as much a way of thinking about doing business, in which careful attention is given to the concept of reciprocity, as it is a technique of doing business. One major objective is thus to show with examples how the most successful companies, many of them American, have improved their chances of success by seriously adopting countertrade in their corporate strategies.

The second objective, to influence policymakers in Washington, arises from a basic proposition that offset, a type of countertrade prevalent in military sales, creates not only strategic opportunities but tough problems that can only be resolved by negotiations between the United States and its trading partners on a government-to-government basis. Countertrade, especially in the area of military offsets or compensating trade required by foreign government policy, makes life miserable and difficult for thousands of businesspeople in the defense industry and other high-tech areas such as telecommunications, where the offset concept is spreading rapidly among foreign countries.

In this chapter I talk about the forces that have caused countertrade to arise in the last few years, the special and alarming problem of military offsets, and the relationships of countertrade to financing.

The third objective, as mentioned in the introductory chapter, is to make the general public understand the nature and importance of countertrade. Countertrade presents enormous opportunities for promoting U.S. export trade, but most Americans have never heard of it.

THE PROBLEM OF OFFSETS

Countertrade in the form of offset makes life difficult for a number of reasons. It forces defense contractors, for example, to export general products such as ham or textiles that they know nothing about, creating extra costs that can inflate the cost of a sale and causing the ironic situation where the U.S. exporter must actually import these products back into the United States when our trade deficit is already worse than ever. Offset also puts the U.S. company in the position of having to transfer technology as part of an offset package even when the company believes a certain transfer is not in its best interest, and may be used in a few years by a Japanese or Italian company to build a competing export. Finally, offsets can require U.S. companies to invest in the creation of whole foreign industries, such as a commercial aircraft factory in China or an F-16 plant in Turkey, to name just two among dozens of examples. The U.S. company considers itself very lucky indeed if such an investment, officially required by a foreign government, is in the business it actually understands. General Dynamics, for example, had to invest in Turkish hotels as well as in the Turkish aircraft industry. It believes it has made sound investments in both cases.

To the Federal legislator in Washington, it would be a natural temptation to introduce legislation restricting the ability of U.S. companies to comply with these offset requests. Nothing could be more damaging to U.S. exporters.

This book, then, urges the Congress and the White House to begin serious negotiations with foreign governments about controlling their requests for offsets, while continuing to allow U.S. companies their current flexibility to provide creative countertrade and offset packages in order to win valuable exports for themselves and for the United

States. Countertrade does have this potential contribution toward resolving our trade deficit. First, by doing counter-trade well and creatively, U.S. companies will continue to win more export sales than otherwise possible. Second, by controlling the foreign governments' appetite for offsets, the United States government can reduce or at least control these add-ons and sweeteners that U.S. exporters are re-quired to give foreign governments, giving back much of the hard-earned export value, the net foreign exchange in the sale.

THE OFFSET CONCEPT

The very word "offset" deals with a critical foreign exchange question. Offsets are the technique by which foreign govern-ments *pull back*, or *offset*, the foreign exchange or hard currency they lose when spending vast sums—for example, to buy fighter aircraft, or an antiaircraft missile system, or a telecommunications system. When Turkey buys F-16s from General Dynamics or when France buys AWACS airborne radar planes from Boeing, they must pay dollars because both manufacturers are American. They write their contracts in dollars and want to be paid in dollars so as not to take what is called a foreign exchange risk by accepting payment in Turkish lira or French francs. Turkey and France get dollars mainly by generating sales of export products, such as Turkish carpets or French wine to the United States. Offsets are a way of getting the U.S. exporter to take on the responsibility of generating some of these exports for France or Turkey, or of doing the foreign exchange equivalent, investing in French or Turkish factories or transferring technology to them. An offset policy says basically that if you want us to spend government money on your export to us, you must export products from our country, co-invest in industry here, or transfer technology to us.

I have initially focused on the offset problem, prevalent in military sales, more than commercial countertrade, which includes all sorts of *linked* trading, or *countertrade* in the nonmilitary area. An important reason for this bias is the large scope and rapid development of military offsets. Offsets have taken on a kind of life of their own and have become a serious issue. They are typically calculated as a percentage of value of the sale itself. When Spain first developed its offset policy in the early 1980s (as discussed in Chapter 5), the typical amount requested was 30 percent. In the mid-1980s, 100 percent was reached in various European purchases, and 1987 transactions such as Boeing's sale of the AWACS to the United Kingdom and France contained 130 percent, 30 percent greater than the sale value itself. Other sales have realized even higher offset values. Since 1975, offsets have become commonplace among virtually all the countries we trade with.

OIL PRICE INCREASES

Why are offsets so widespread? Why have military offsets in particular spread so quickly when the practice was virtually unheard of before 1975? One reason for the phenomenon is the dramatic increase in oil prices by the Organization of Petroleum Exporting Countries (OPEC) in the early 1970s. Oil importing nations (i.e., much of the world) were suddenly spending far greater amounts for oil and had to become more resourceful about generating foreign exchange through exports, to pay for the oil. The oil price increases are believed to have helped in part to accelerate commercial, nonmilitary countertrade. Certainly, this appears to be true in South America where the incidence of commercial countertrade, and the rapid creation of countertrade policy for all importing, parallels the debt crisis on that continent, a crisis no doubt accelerated by rising oil bills. In another example of the same basic problem, the African republic of Madagascar, virtually bankrupt and out of credit, resorted to trading cloves in order to complete the construction of a badly needed fertilizer plant. This commercial countertrade transaction, essentially a barter, is discussed more fully in Chapter 8.

Even the Eastern Bloc countries, where countertrade was prevalent before the oil price increases, have had to scramble to adjust. A significant part of their trade with the Soviet Union, for example, is built on the swapping of numerous manufactured goods out of Eastern Europe for Soviet oil.

All forms of countertrade in the world accelerate where oil prices increase. This parallel occurrence suggests a fundamental: Countertrade flourishes when money is scarce. When oil sops up government budgets, less money is available to be spent elsewhere. The recent rise of countertrade is thus an ominous index of world economic disruption. Countertrade feeds off huge trade imbalances and wildly fluctuating currencies, as national economies pitch and yaw, desperately seeking some greater level of stability and equilibrium. Countertrade is also a positive development because it permits sales, and therefore trade balance adjustments, to occur between countries even when their currencies are nonconvertible or money is scarce.

OTHER FACTORS CAUSING COUNTERTRADE

It would be wrong, however, to lay all the blame for offset and commercial countertrade on oil price increases. Other factors have caused money to become scarce and counter-trade to flourish. The economic and political isolation that makes the currencies of Eastern Europe unconvertible facili-tates countertrade in the region. A more complex factor is the rise of industrial and high-tech competitors in many nations outside the United States. Without several com-peting international companies, military offset require-ments generally, and the commercial countertrade policies of Latin America, for example, could not be imposed on companies quite so easily by governments. Turkey could not have required such a large offset on General Dynamics' F-16 sale without less costly (and less effective) alternatives having been available from British Aerospace and the French aerospace companies, Aerospatiale and Dassault. In short, competition helps to make offset work as a sweet-ener to a foreign government. The message is: No compli-ance, no sale. The buyer will award this bid to your competitor or will decide not to purchase your products at all.

Another factor lies behind the certain and steady rise of the military and high-tech offset concept (and to a lesser extent, commercial countertrade). It works, all too well! Japan, Australia, and Canada, and every country in Europe have all created dozens of companies and even whole indus-tries using the offset concept of requiring that a seller balance a sale with a commitment to transfer technology and invest in that country. There are numerous examples: the develop-ment of a German tank industry in Switzerland (Leopard II) and of a U.S. Raytheon missile in Italy (Aspide), and the latest F-16 sale to Japan, where Mitsubishi will redesign American blueprints under license and cram a U.S. shell with Japanese electronics. General Dynamics has no choice but to transfer significant technology in this latter sale and to agree to a co-production scheme for the plane. They would have lost out to another U.S. or European maker, or to a consortium of Japanese companies.

Perhaps the greatest proof that offsets work beautifully is the proliferation of this policy among the strongest Asian economies (Japan, South Korea, and Singapore), not just among the lesser developed Asian economies (Indonesia and the People's Republic of China).

The jury is still out on whether general trading commitments under offsets will work as well as the technology transfer and investment parts of an offset obligation. Companies attempt to put the cost of trading in the price of a sale, despite the buyer's best efforts to monitor the transaction and prevent this from happening. Nevertheless, there are many clear examples—ham traded from Yugoslavia by McDonnell-Douglas, machine tools traded from Switzerland by Northrop, among others—where the goods were in oversupply and might not have been traded except through an offset.

ALTERNATIVE FINANCING

Another important aspect of countertrade is that it should be viewed as a kind of financing, indeed an alternative financing. Like government-subsidized export credit financing, countertrade is both a financing weapon and an arena of competition where companies battle each other to win the ultimate export sale. It is hard to view countertrade in the sense of military offsets, and even much of commercial countertrade, outside the context of government-subsidized financing schemes. The United States is being hard pressed by offsets, but is even harder pressed by the financing schemes of foreign governments.

Using countertrade effectively is important to U.S. corporations because they often need a large offset package to compensate for their lack of an attractive financing package when bidding for a sale against foreign competition. If a foreign export sale is substantial enough to require an offset, it is often going to be financed by government export credit as well. This is especially the case in Third World countries, but has also been true in Spain, Turkey, and Portugal. In the late 1970s, the U.S. Eximbank stopped making loans to the most highly developed countries, e.g., Japan and West Germany. Such countries do not normally finance sales to one another with government export credit, even though they may require offsets.

The exporter from Europe or Japan will *almost always* go into the bidding for such a large sale with a better financing package available to it than a U.S. company! Most businesspeople from major U.S. corporations understand this as a given, yet many officials in Congress and the executive branch, tragically, do not understand it. U.S. companies know that in larger international export sales that require medium- or long-term financing of three or more years, such as missile systems, military aircraft, or turnkey factories, the foreign competitor can count on subsidized export credit (i.e., lower than market rates and longer terms) from its government to finance the bid. Normal market interest rates in the exporting powers, West Germany, Japan, and Switzerland, are already lower than the prime rate in the United States, giving them a certain advantage. When companies from these countries are bidding on a sale and are backed by even better government export credit terms, the foreign companies become tough competition indeed for the United States. The bottom line is that when a company from overseas (even outside of West Germany, Japan, or Switzerland) is backed by export credit, the competing U.S.

company stands a very good chance of losing unless it can get financing from one of three principal U.S. financing entities: Foreign Military Sales (FMS) credits from the Defense Security Assistance Agency (DSAA), a State Department agency based in the Pentagon; the U.S. Export-Import Bank (Eximbank); or the Agency for International Development (AID) within the State Department.*

EXIMBANK

These agencies did not fare well during President Reagan's Administration, when the trade deficit more than quadrupled from $30–40 billion levels to over $160 billion. Eximbank's lending programs were sharply cut back from levels that exceeded $4 billion annually under the Carter Administration to under $500 million annually during the Reagan Administration, with the legal authorization level lowered to $690 million by 1988. When the strong, overvalued dollar is added to the lack of aggressive government financing during the first six Reagan years, these two factors alone go part of the distance in explaining the shocking increase in the U.S. trade deficit. They are part of the "structural" problem underlying the U.S. trade deficit and have as much to do with it, I believe, as so-called "management," "quality" issues, and "cost of labor" issues.

It is important to understand that Eximbank loans and guarantees are normally made in combination with commercial bank credit and thus have far greater potential to stimulate and facilitate exports than the actual dollar value of the loan.

*I am focusing here on manufactured goods, not agricultural products, and thus have not mentioned the Commodity Credit Corporation (CCC) of the United States government, administered by the Agriculture Department.

Table 1   DIRECT CREDIT AUTHORIZATIONS OF THE U.S. EXPORT–IMPORT BANK, 1978–1987 (millions of dollars)

1978	$2,870
1979	3,700
1980	4,900
1981	5,000
1982	3,100
1983	685
1984	1,100
1985	320
1986	370
1987	410

Source: Eximbank.

Table 1 shows the decrease of Eximbank's direct lending programs from 1978 through 1987, from the Carter Administration through the Reagan Administration. Eximbank defines its direct loans as extensions of credit from its own funds for exports of larger than $5 million, at terms of longer than five years. Usually guaranteed by the central bank of the borrowing country, these loans are critical for larger exports in competitive situations involving, for example, power plants and turnkey factories. To be fair, market conditions accounted for some decrease in Eximbank programs during the 1980s; foreign orders for U.S. nuclear plant exports, often supported by Eximbank direct credits, dried up after 1979; and direct credits were no longer needed to finance commercial aircraft after an accord with France in 1982. Aircraft direct lending was replaced with guarantees of commercial bank loans. However, all Eximbank programs including direct credits and short- to medium-term guarantees and insurance, did fall sharply during the Reagan years as part of conscious policy and have not been replaced.

The shrinking of Eximbank is but one example of a philosophy of *laissez-faire* practiced recently by the United States government in the field of export trade. This philosophy has left U.S. exporters at the mercy of two major forms of foreign government intervention on behalf of their own exporters: offsets and aggressive export financing.

ELIMINATING THE U.S. TRADE DEFICIT

An important goal of this book is to shine light on this fact: Foreign official requests for countertrade and foreign export credit intervention have gone essentially unanswered by the United States government. Some major building of exports has to occur if the U.S. trade deficit is to be eliminated. To maximize exports generally, the United States will need a comprehensive trade policy using tools such as an offset policy, adequate export financing from government sources, and even tax incentives, among other measures. A reinvigorated Commerce Department is needed to lead this effort.

As the Japanese have recently demonstrated, powerful exporting not only has economic benefits but enables a country to project influence. Certainly, exporting has helped the U.S. project its influence in the past and can do so in the future. Even the Russians, in Eastern Europe, and the Chinese, in the Middle East, are finding that their exports project and strengthen policies of interaction.

No one factor, such as a strong dollar, accounts for the huge trade deficit buildup in the United States, and a weaker dollar, by itself, will not correct our trade deficit. An active countertrade policy and aggressive export financing can function as tools in a coherent U.S. trade policy.

The argument is sometimes made that cheap labor overseas is the major cause for our trade deficit. The world had plenty of cheap labor during the Carter Administration too, but U.S. exporters of large manufactured goods, such as Caterpillar tractors, seem to have fared better then than during the 1980s. The U.S. trade deficit kept increasing during the Reagan presidency, even when oil prices finally broke and fell by more than half, and the oil bill part of our trade deficit stabilized.

President Carter's economic policies certainly had short-comings. The grain embargo in 1980, a policy designed to protest the Russian invasion of Afghanistan, brought millions of tons of wheat business to our allies and had little effect on the Russians. However, Eximbank under its chairman John L. Moore, Jr. had a kind of activist approach to financing during the Carter Administration. This approach will have to be emulated and probably surpassed as part of a new, comprehensive effort to resolve our trade deficit. The Moore approach was to match foreign subsidized financing offers by aggressively using adjustments in interest rates, length of term, and percentage of cover, without going below the interest rate floor established by the U.S. Treasury through its lending window to Eximbank, the Federal Financing Bank (FFB). This floor usually prevented Eximbank from matching truly concessional aid financing and grant funds extended by foreign governments, but it did allow Eximbank to compete with the financing packages offered by its direct competitors, Japan's Eximbank, Coface in France, Hermes in West Germany, and ECGD in the United Kingdom, among others.

Eximbank in those years tried hard to make the financing package "not a factor," as Moore sometimes put it, so that bids could be evaluated in terms of price. In its most active years under Moore, Eximbank was financing nearly 20 percent of all U.S. manufactured goods and 7 percent of all U.S. exports (with agricultural commodities added). U.S.

companies still lost business when foreign government financing was under the minimal constraints permitted Eximbank. In addition, Eximbank was expressly forbidden by law from financing military exports. There was also a tradition, understood by Eximbank and by congressional oversight, that Eximbank could not mix highly concessional aid (and grant) financing in its packages. Military financing was to be left to Foreign Military Sales and concessional aid financing to AID. On a few occasions, Moore's Eximbank offered aid-equivalent financing below its cost of funds from the FFB, and the U.S. bidder still lost when the foreign financing was better.

Knowing they face a tough fight to get government financing from Eximbank, FMS, and AID forces the large U.S. exporters to place the manufacturing with their foreign subsidiaries in order to get attractive financing from Eximbank's counterpart in the subsidiaries' own country. People who do not work for large U.S. exporting companies may find this hard to believe because so many jobs are lost to the United States in this fashion. Yet it happens all the time. Increasingly, U.S. companies develop an attractive countertrade package as well, to complement the best financing available from an overseas source. (The Zimbabwe–Rockwell printing press transaction discussed in Chapter 7 is not atypical. To win against stiff French competition, Rockwell manufactured this export in its British subsidiary in order to get attractive export credit financing from Britain's export financing agency, ECGD. On top of this, Rockwell offered the purchaser, Zimbabwe, 100 percent offset as well, by agreeing to purchase the value of the press, $7 million, in minerals from its mines.)

A major conceptual and philosophical problem has prevented the United States government from having an activist, flexible export credit policy and from developing the kind of countertrade policy commonplace among *all* our trading partners. It is a lack of pragmatism and of a will to live realistically in the competitive conditions of international trade as it exists today. To our allies, government financing and government offset requirements are as natural as breathing air; they are extended without a lot of fundamental questioning.

If the United States does increase export financing, some Europeans are bound to complain that we are undermining their market share. However, European finance officials would probably applaud a more stable dollar, even if it is brought about by a more active U.S. export policy. The example of the Blohm & Voss shipbuilding company illustrates how even a West German manufacturer actively sought United States government financing to support the U.S. content of a West German sale to Turkey. Blohm & Voss lobbied for it directly at the Pentagon because in this case U.S. companies were large subcontractors. Their inability to get FMS financing from the Pentagon concerned the West Germans, who knew the Turkish Navy badly wanted U.S. equipment on two new frigates, complementing four already built. The shipbuilder feared the lack of U.S. financing might kill its own prime contract too, if the Turkish Navy soured on a deal without U.S. content.

When Blohm & Voss wanted to finance the four initial frigates for sale to Turkey in the early 1980s, they ran up against credit problems common for that country. West Germany's banks and military lending facility already had so much Turkish risk they could not take on any more. In the United States, such a problem would have killed the sale. In West Germany, the government made an exception, allowing its export credit agency (Hermes) to get involved, something still not possible in the United States. Blohm & Voss won the sale. At least some U.S. subcontractors were beneficiaries of the German prime contract by providing components to the frigates.

When the French badly want a sale, they use a finance concept they invented called *credit mix*, in which concessional export credit is blended with highly concessional aid credits (or even grants), including low interest rates of 2–6 percent, long grace periods of one or more years, and long repayment terms. The Japanese have perfected this mixing of government financing sources to an art form. Even though Congress has made it easier to match the *credit mix*, there is still neither the will nor the structure to mix all of our financing instruments with the ease and success of our trading partners.

WHAT IS WRONG?

It is not easy to answer this question. Our current notion of the free market, where government support is still considered a "bad thing," may be unrealistic and a little naïve. The kind of free market that propelled the United States to become an economic power in the first half of this century does not exist today for Japan, West Germany, the rest of Europe, the emerging Asian powers, or even Canada and Australia. These trading partners blend government financing instruments, require military offsets, and focus overall trade policy into a relatively coherent set of objectives and instruments. Basically, they all now do something we have done only in wartime—make the ability to manufacture and to ship goods overseas in almost "do or die" fashion a national security issue of gravest importance.

EXPORT CREDIT

The issue of government export credit deserves book-length discussions in its own right but is vital as background for understanding the context in which offset and countertrade occur. Both are motivated by government desire to intervene in trade and to tip the balance in its own favor on a sale or purchase. Even away from offset in the area of commercial countertrade, the typical transaction initiated by a company requires foreign government intervention, often as the approval of one or more government ministries. I am not recommending that the U.S. Eximbank try to finance our way out of the trade deficit by making overly risky loans and supplanting commercial bank credit. By lending carefully, as it has done in the past, Eximbank does have a much stronger role to play. Reducing the barriers in competitive situations among Eximbank, AID, and FMS might not hurt our trade effort either. Actually, in the late 1970s, the U.S. money center banks welcomed the activist Eximbank position because it generated more business for them. Even if the role of large commercial banks was confined merely to the downpayment portion of a loan, it was significant business that would not have happened except for Eximbank's participation.

A few prominent Republican policymakers believe that budget cutters in the White House and Congress may have acted too zealously in cutting Eximbank's programs at a time when all of our trading partners were looking for ways to maintain or to intensify both their export credit and their countertrade programs, seeking to erode our market position and to make it difficult for us to get it back. Former ambassador to Yugoslavia Larry Eagleburger (Henry Kissinger's protégé and a former Under Secretary of State for Policy) has long been a public champion of Eximbank lending, having seen the critical position it played in financing U.S. sales in Yugoslavia.

One of the most aggressive lenders ever to serve as chairman of Eximbank was none other than William ("Bill")

Casey, the former CIA Director, who won the hearts of American conservatives by allegedly making it possible for Lieutenant Colonel Oliver North to develop the Iran Contra connection. Casey was chairman of Eximbank under President Nixon and was revered by much of its staff for his aggressive, "interventionist," damn-the-torpedoes style.

Actually, Eximbank's congressional appropriation was once, during the late Nixon–Ford years, not even put into the budget, for a simple, sound reason. Eximbank made a profit while performing its valuable service. Loans outstanding were in the process of being repaid. In this sense, it seemed rather whimisical when David Stockman argued in the early 1980s that Eximbank's budget appropriation should be cut, because the budget cutting process was going to affect the people and their social programs and therefore should hurt the exporting corporations too. He and his colleagues succeeded in this objective, and a huge trade deficit is in part their legacy.

United States presidents have paid little attention either to Eximbank or to trade policy, delegating influence on both to the chairman of Eximbank and to cabinet officers. The result has been wild fluctuations in Eximbank lending levels, making it highly undependable as our allies, backed by dependable export credit, steadily chipped away at our export markets. Under Republican presidents, different Eximbank chairmen have pursued policies ranging from minimal to aggressive lending. The two Nixon chairmen, Bill Casey and Henry Kearns, took an activist approach to direct lending. William Draper, who was the first of Reagan's two chairmen, and Steve DuBrul, Ford's chairman, came close to dismantling Eximbank's direct lending programs in favor of commercial bank guarantees from Eximbank. Such loans are often not competitive if the foreign manufacturer is supported with a low-interest loan from its government. The guarantee approach still does not allow the commercial bank making a loan under the guarantee to lower its interest rate enough to be competitive.

Ironically, Japan and the richer developing countries such as Korea, India, and Brazil have patterned their export credit agencies after the U.S. Eximbank, and are in several cases seeking to surpass the United States in financing trade. The countries that have these banks, including our European friends, are in any event now actively building their programs. I hope that we will not be left behind in the field of export credit, in countertrade, or in trade policy itself.

A more detailed example helps to illustrate the role of government export credit and countertrade in the ebb and flow of putting a sale together. The frigate program to the Turkish Navy, though military in nature, was financed largely through Hermes-backed export credit in the early 1980s. Military offsets were not required by the Turkish authorities at the time of the initial German prime contract. Conditions in Turkey changed quickly. Turkey requested offsets for the prime contractor for the two follow-on frigates. As a critical North Atlantic Treaty Organization (NATO) and U.S. ally, with borders on Iran, Iraq, Syria, the Soviet Union, and Bulgaria, Turkey began to upgrade its military substantially and to request offsets more frequently to help compensate for its increased spending. Turkish authorities are impressed by the large offset package being implemented by General Dynamics (GD), discussed in Chapter 3, in connection with its F-16 fighter aircraft. Investments and some trading have already occurred under the offset program. In addition, the Turkish aerospace project, begun with GD co-investment in 1984, has now manufactured the first F-16 in Turkey.

The F-16 program introduced another economic change in Turkey. Since much of this program is financed under the Pentagon's FMS credits (with some grant funds as well), it takes up a major part of the FMS credit available for Turkey over a ten-year period. FMS credits for FY 1987 and FY 1988 have been frozen at $490 million annually. This means no FMS credits will be available to start a new purchase program in Turkey from a U.S. company, unless Congress raises the appropriation for Turkish financing significantly above the annual $490 million level. There is currently no way for U.S. defense contractors to get export credit from the United States for their sales to Turkey, even though the Turkish government is developing plans to make several major purchases from international competitors.

To pursue a subcontract role in the Turkish frigate program, I flew with my client to Hamburg, West Germany. We drove from the Atlantic Kempenski Hotel, with its vast rooms and 15-foot ceilings, to the Blohm & Voss shipyard. It was an eerie feeling to be driving through a prosperous city that had been severely bombed in World War II, heading for a meeting with the very shipbuilder that produced Germany's famous *Bismarck*, the super-battleship that was eventually sunk in that war.

We learned in the meeting that, once again, Hermes would make an exception and provide financing for the frigates. An offset request was expected, and plans were being developed to have a German trading company fulfill it. Blohm & Voss said there was a chance that the Hermes government financing could be extended for the U.S. content in the project, but that we should not count on it. German authorities would probably insist on local content if German financing were used. The Blohm & Voss officials knew the Turkish Navy wanted U.S. equipment, and had already visited the Pentagon to request financing support to please their Turkish customer. Blohm & Voss warned, however, that they already had German and Italian suppliers and financing lined up. If the Pentagon failed to offer an FMS credit or guarantee, U.S. suppliers would be quickly pulled from the sale and replaced with German and Italian suppliers.

In Turkey on a later trip, it was proposed that some U.S. equipment be financed through barter, and the Turks listened with interest. No one had ever proposed any kind of trading concept to support a sale before, and the Turks were looking to some of their major importing companies to generate more exports. Our idea was to have a trading company accept Turkish lira and use this local currency to buy commodities such as wheat, barley, and cotton, which could be traded out and sold on the international market for foreign exchange. This money would be built up in an evidence account and used to pay U.S. suppliers. Turkish officials in the Finance and Treasury Ministry responded that one could now buy dollars with lira locally for the first time in years. While our barter scheme was no longer really necessary to deal with the Turkish lira's lack of convertibility, our willingness to do trading was considered interesting, even a breakthrough. It might help the Turkish officials to secure more local budget authority to use in purchasing U.S. equipment, alleviating some of the bureaucratic in-fighting needed to secure more dollar budget authority.

At the meeting, Turkish Navy officials described the trading ideas as helpful but announced, quite unexpectedly, that Pentagon FMS funds had been squeezed out of some other programs and were going to be made available. We left the country believing that unless something new happened, the sudden appearance of FMS would make our sale go through.

FRUSTRATING TASK

In many ways, writing about countertrade and the related problem of export credit can be very frustrating. I have searched for ways to make the subject understandable, asking myself, Why does a subject of this importance have to be so complex? While foreign trade has always been important to the United States, many of our manufacturers benefited from the huge U.S. domestic market. Sears Roebuck, for example, remained very loyal to its U.S. suppliers, even when the dollar was at its strongest and could have purchased many more goods from overseas for sale in its huge store network. The total percentage of overseas sourcing at Sears has remained quite modest.

Many people with great public knowledge claim that Americans do not care about the trade deficit, or trade, or the lack of an American trade policy, let alone countertrade and export credit. Unemployment is at the lowest level in years, inflation is under control. Why should people be concerned? Should our government be worried?

Felix Rohatyn, the New York investment banker, found an effective way to answer this question and to dramatize the trade deficit issue in a recent speech.[4] The falling dollar, brought on by the deficit, and the strong Japanese stock market combine to give Fuji Bank a market value of $60 billion, ten times the value of Morgan Guaranty Trust in New York. Toyota's value of $40 billion contrasts with Chrysler's value of $4 billion. Think of how easy it would be for Japanese corporations and investors to buy up key U.S. companies, technology, and real estate. In Tokyo, and in other foreign capitals, the new American gold rush has already begun.

Promoting and building U.S. exports are still the best ways to balance this situation and to strengthen the U.S. dollar to a firmer, more realistic level. Such export development has the added advantage of creating more jobs in the United States. Export promotionism is still the best alternative to protectionism!

Chapter Three

Fighter Aircraft
for Hotels:
The Case of Turkey

*"You must take your offset commitment
seriously, from top management including the
chairman throughout the organization,
or you are going to fail."*
—CARY VIKTOR, Director of International Offsets—Capital Projects, General
Dynamics Corporation

GENERAL DYNAMICS SHOWS HOW!

General Dynamics (GD) makes the F-16 jet aircraft, the Trident submarine, the M-1 Tank, and the Stinger over-the-shoulder missile. GD is probably the best known defense contractor in the United States and has developed successful export sales around the world. The most successful export, the F-16 aircraft, has been sold in multibillion-dollar transactions to some of America's most important allies— South Korea, Greece, Turkey, and a consortium of NATO allies including Norway, Denmark, Belgium, and the Netherlands, among others. In every one of these sales the purchasing country received a major offset package to help it resolve the domestic political and economic problems caused by such a large military purchase.

Just what is involved in an offset package? To answer that question, this chapter is about GD's offset program in Turkey. Most companies that make a large offset commitment have a division or department to execute and carry out that commitment. In GD, this department is run by Joe Serrano. A key member of Joe's staff is a former colleague of mine, Cary Viktor.

Before promotion to his current job, Cary commuted to Turkey every month for two and a half years. In the course of that time he met the chairman of every top company in the country and briefed the prime minister several times. Turkey obviously took the offset program seriously. Fortunately, so did GD.

OFFSET COMMITMENT IN TURKEY

At first glance, the GD offset commitment in Turkey is daunting (see Table 2). The sale itself was enormous: 160

F-16s at a cost of $4.2 billion in 1983, sold to Turkey for cash and a Foreign Military Sales (FMS) loan from the Pentagon. Against this, a direct offset commitment of $150 million was signed on May 11, 1984, committing GD to

Table 2 GENERAL DYNAMICS' OFFSET COMMITMENT IN TURKEY—1984

Sale

160 F-16s sold to Turkey:	$4.2 billion (1983)

Offset

1. Direct offset of related defense and electronic components to be exported from Turkey, including training: $150 million

2. Indirect offset to be fulfilled by investment and exports of nondefense general products: $1.27 billion

   A. General Dynamics: $800.5 million
   B. Radar subcontractor
      Westinghouse: $52 million
   C. Engine subcontractor
      General Electric: $317.5 million

3. Creation of new aerospace industry facility in Turkey, Tusas to assemble and co-produce F-16s through technology transfer.

Total capital investment required:	$137 million
General Dynamics:	$58 million
General Electric:	$9 million
Government of Turkey:	$68 million
Turkish Air Force Foundation and Turkish Air League:	$2 million

TOTALS:

General Dynamics:	$1,008.5 million
General Electric:	$326 million
Westinghouse:	$152 million

Courtesy of General Dynamics.

purchase components in Turkey's aerospace program directly or to provide training in it. On November 9, 1984, GD signed an indirect offset commitment, agreeing to provide services and to export products from Turkey unrelated to the F-16 or the aerospace program.

In addition, GD committed to fund and set up a new aerospace company, Tusas (pronounced tusash) Aerospace Industries, Inc. (TAI). The purpose of this company, housed in a large, newly constructed factory, is to assemble and co-produce the F-16 in Turkey, and to provide support for the program including research development, design, training, and servicing. GD set up this company as a joint venture with Turkey and its principal subcontractor, General Electric Corporation (GE), which makes the engines. Of the $137 million required to capitalize the project, GD put in $58 million (42%), GE funded $9 million (7%), Turkey put in $68 million (49%), and the Turkish Airforce Foundation and Turkish Air League put in the remaining $2 million (2%). The company, Tusas, was thus 51 percent Turkish owned and 49 percent U.S. owned.

The Turkish government allowed GD to spend the $150 million direct offset commitment on the development of a whole town around the TAI complex. This included housing for 2,000 personnel to work in the plant and training for them, as well as a hospital, mosque, school, waste treatment plant, power plant, and roads. In addition to assembling the F-16s, TAI is manufacturing in Turkey the aft fuselage, center fuselage, and wings. The rest of the components are being shipped in. The first plane rolled off the assembly line in October of 1987, ahead of schedule.

As with the creation of TAI, GD requested support for the offset commitment from its principal subcontractors, GE (making the engines) and Westinghouse (providing the radar). GD has overall responsibility for the $1.27 billion indirect offset but was able to sign separate commitments with GE for $317.5 million (25%) and with Westinghouse for $152 million (12%). The performance period is for ten years with a three-year grace period, which means that the offset is to be completed by 1994 or, with the grace period, by 1997. There is a complex penalty formula for noncompliance. A review period every two years is provided to smooth out the process, so that GD does not arrive at the end with a lot of the commitment left uncompleted.

In total, GD's obligation in Turkey for the F-16 is $1,008.5 million. This is a huge sum in absolute terms but represents a relatively modest 24 percent of the actual contract value. The offset figure in some more recent military sales to European countries, such as France and the United Kingdom, has easily exceeded 100 percent.

GUIDELINES FOR INDIRECT OFFSET

Initially, the government laid down guidelines for the indirect offset, asking GD to fulfill 90 percent of it through the procurement and export of Turkish products and 10 percent through capital investment and the promotion of tourism in Turkey. When GD began to look around for products to export from Turkey, such as cotton, textiles, and orange juice concentrate, they found the process difficult, time-consuming, and expensive. GD could get only one dollar of offset credit for each dollar of product exported. In 1984 and 1985, as the development of TAI got underway, the Turkish authorities began to have a change of heart. They came to believe that investment was worth more to them because of its inherent leverage. Since dollars invested in an industry (e.g., a hotel) could generate far more cash than the original investment sum, Turkey began to encourage GD to invest more, even to reverse the percentage under the guidelines with 90 percent now to be fulfilled by investment. The encouragement Turkey provided was to award GD offset credit based on a multiplier formula. GD thus receives offset credit, to be negotiated in each case, of several times the value of its actual investment. The leverage could be further increased since GD could use its reputation and network to enlist the support of investment partners.

INDIRECT INVESTMENT

Under Cary Viktor's guidance, the first indirect investment was in the Ankara Hilton Hotel, to be followed by three more, one each in Izmir, a port in the west; in Mersin, a port in the south; and in Istanbul on the Bosphorus. (Istanbul also has the original Hilton in the country.) GD's investment in each hotel is $2 million with additional equity put in by foreign and local partners. The advantage to GD, if these projects work as planned, is that its money will generate a cash flow and eventually a profit once the investment is paid back.

GD has put together another investment project in Turkey with Bechtel, the giant U.S. engineering and construction firm based in San Francisco. GD will invest about $20 million in a billion-dollar thermal power plant project. Bechtel will lead the construction but will be joined on a subcontract basis by other investment partners, Combustion Engineering of the United States, Siemens of West Germany, Royal Dutch Shell, and either a Korean or a Japanese company. GD expects to get $250–300 million in offset credit for this project, and the government will guarantee a 15–20 percent return on investment.

SUBCONTRACTORS

GD has been able to get additional offset credit from a countertrade arrangement with Rockwell, the Pittsburgh-based defense and aerospace contractor. As part of its subcontract arrangement with GD on the M-1 tank, Rockwell agreed to help out with offset wherever it could through its own project development. Rockwell had independently agreed to an automotive brake plant investment in Turkey but succeeded in getting offset credit for this project assigned to GD, partially fulfilling its own commitment to GD as a subcontractor for the tank program.

As it turned out, GD is fulfilling its offset primarily through investment and technology transfer projects, while exports have thus far played a minor role. The government does not seem to mind because GD has been very creative in designing investment strategies as well as bringing in partners.

GD is currently working on a plan to fund the transfer of some unclassified Stinger missile parts to the Turkish electronics company Aselsan. Components will be made by Aselsan as a function of how many missiles Turkey buys from GD, but offset credit would still be awarded. Other components of the missile would be purchased in Greece, Italy, and West Germany, depending on how many missiles these countries buy as well. The German defense contractor, Dornier, would assemble the missile in West Germany with components shipped in from the subcontracting countries. GD is given credit not only for the technology transferred and funded to Aselsan, but for the missile component exports from Turkey as well. In the broader picture, GD is able to use the offset concept to build a market for the Stinger.

Cary is also looking at investing in some agribusiness projects in Turkey with Land O'Lakes and ConAgra from the United States. He is considering a project to finish and export Turkish marble, pointing out that a lot of "Italian" marble is actually mined in Turkey and finished in Italy.

OFFSET WILL WORK!

The oldest of GD's investment projects is no more than three years old. Time will tell whether Cary's approach to offset will work; all of the projects are too recent to have begun to produce a cash flow. However, many people inside and outside the company believe the approach will work beautifully. The benefits are manifold. Offset credit is built up quickly, strengthening the overall long-term relationship with programs of great benefit to the country. GD is able to use the offset skillfully to expand its exports and programs in Turkey and elsewhere. Finally, GD stands to make a return from its investments, which have been carefully partnered to spread the risk, to increase the leverage, and to build valuable new relationships both inside and outside the country.

In 1985, GD's offset unit generated $75.5 million in indirect offset credit and in 1986, $190 million. A figure of over $200 million is projected for 1987. So far, GD's overall approach has cost the company less than four cents for each dollar of offset credit fulfilled. GD may end up in a lot of businesses it never planned to enter but at least they appear to be profitable, and more important still, the company's core defense business has been strengthened. In the process, GD has been able to avoid hiring a trading company to develop exports, as is sometimes done in fulfilling offset requirements. They have not paid any trading commissions or consultant fees. They did not have to subsidize general exports by purchasing them at below market prices in order to sell them elsewhere in the world.

The staff that manages GD's indirect offset programs is surprisingly small and was established only in early 1985. At the St. Louis headquarters, there are seven management people including Cary. Staff are located in Turkey, Korea, Belgium, and Greece, where major offset programs are underway. The division is considered a service to the corporation, not a profit center. The offset group often teams with a specially designated person in an operating division to develop offset strategy and to avoid a duplication of effort. A lot of collaboration is required if the offset is to work effectively. When the division was set up, the chairman sent a letter throughout the company asking everyone to take offset obligations seriously. The letter stressed the importance of such a corporate-wide commitment by top management and emphasized the need to communicate the decision, reinforcing it with action. The persistent attention of management has been critical to the offset department's success and is a hopeful sign in a major corporation that, like the United States, needs more exports to grow.

Chapter Four

Military Offsets, A European Tyranny

*"We use offset agreements as
door openers to tear down
'Buy American' restrictions."*
—Swiss Embassy Official, Washington, D.C.

OVERVIEW

The practice by foreign governments of requesting compensating offsets in military sales is far more widespread than most people realize. It is critical for the United States government and Congress not to restrict, in any way, U.S. companies' ability to win export sales by concluding offset agreements, except to review technology transfer agreements for national security concerns. The brunt of congressional and White House outrage should be directed not at U.S. companies struggling skillfully to sell valuable exports, but at foreign governments, our NATO allies, and especially France, who are extracting huge offset commitments from the United States with zeal and greed.

In December 1985, the U.S. Office of Management and Budget surveyed offset obligations being accepted by U.S. corporations to facilitate their export sales. The 212 corporations surveyed for the years 1980–1984 took on offset commitments of a staggering $12 billion in order to make sales of $22 billion. In foreign exchange terms, we were giving back about half of what we sold, or giving a discount of about 50 percent. Most of these sales were of defense-related aircraft, engines, and electronics to NATO countries or other allies with whom we have special security arrangements.

The small number of national buyers and large number of manufacturers in the United States and worldwide create a buyer's market in which U.S. corporations have to offer attractive offset packages or simply not be competitive. But the offset requirements of foreign governments introduce major inefficiencies because sales are often made on the basis of the offset package rather than the product sold. (One frustrated U.S. embassy official who sent me the OMB report wrote beside the latter point: "I wish we could convince my host country of this.") Yet there are some benefits: Some sale is better than no sale; some standardization of NATO and other allies' defense forces is achieved; 62,000 new job opportunities created in the United States might otherwise have been lost (see Table 3, pp. 66–67).[2]

U.S. POLICY

It is important in this highly competitive environment that U.S. companies are still winning significant sales and that even with the cost of fulfilling all these offset obligations, U.S. jobs are being created. This is being attained despite negative positions taken by key agencies of the United States government. Deputy Secretary of Defense Charles Duncan in a memorandum dated May 4, 1978 noted the increase in offset requests for military sales. He concluded that unless critical national security interests called for U.S. participation, the Department of Defense should stay out of these agreements, leaving them to the private sector. Additional guidelines set out by the Defense Security Assistance Agency (DSAA) made it more difficult to have Foreign Military Sales (FMS) loans or grants in connection with offsets. DSAA's policy of October 1985 "discouraged" loan financing "for purchases containing offset provisions as a condition for securing the purchase."

History

The widespread practice of requesting offsets in military sales has a fairly recent history. Co-production of U.S. weapons in foreign countries did not begin until the 1950s, with the T-33 aircraft in Japan. The first consciously structured offset sale took place in 1972 with Australia. This was an overall structure rather than a specific transaction. The United States signed a "Memorandum of Discussion," agreeing to facilitate Australian exports up to 25 percent of the value of military exports from the United States into Australia. According to a representative from the Australian embassy, the United States government agreed to inform U.S. companies seeking to export to Australia under FMS credits about the existence of Australia's offset policies. To the extent that U.S. companies fell short in meeting the 25 percent commitment, the United States also agreed on a nonbinding and "best efforts" basis to direct some Pentagon procurement to Australia, provided the Australian products met competitive standards.

In 1975, there were two major offset transactions that set a precedent for future transactions and popularized the idea with European countries: One was the purchase of the General Dynamics (GD) F-16 by a consortium of European countries; the other was the Swiss purchase of Northrop's F-5.

The F-16 purchase by Norway, Denmark, Belgium, and the Netherlands was accomplished mainly through a co-production arrangement. They agreed to purchase $2.8 billion of F-16s in return for co-production in the Netherlands of 10 percent of the value of the initial U.S. Air Force purchase of 650 aircraft, 15 percent of the value of all third-country F-16 purchases from the United States, and 40 percent of the value of their own purchases from the United States.

It is interesting that the offset movement did not get started in Europe until after OPEC sharply increased the price of oil in 1973. It is likely that European governments, faced with large oil bills in dollars, became much more sensitive about major expenditures of dollars even for important defense items. Such huge expenditures also involved the

loss of jobs and technology development as domestic companies were inevitably passed over when the foreign government decided to buy from the United States. Offset was an
obvious way to get hard currency, jobs, and technology
transferred back into Europe, solving both economic and
political problems.

Unlike the NATO consortium, the Swiss decided to limit
co-production of the F-5 and so, for the first time in Europe,
requested offsets beyond co-production. These offsets included Swiss-manufactured goods (mainly machine tools and
electronic components) to be valued at 30 percent of the
$400 million contract price and to be exported by Northrop
over an eight-year term. Werner Kaelin, the Swiss Defense
Procurement Counsellor, explained the offset arrangement to
me. After five years, Northrop had exported only a small
amount of the commitment (about $21 million), understand-
ably experiencing some difficulty with this new offset concept. An agreement was reached in 1980 to extend the
eight-year term of the agreement until mid-1987. A second
series of F-5 purchases began in 1980/1981 with the offset
commitment raised from 30 to 50 percent of the contract
value.

By this time, the United States government had become
troubled by its defense-related offset agreements. In 1977, an
offset department was established in the Pentagon Office of
International Acquisitions, now an agency of the Deputy
Secretary of Defense for Procurement. Its purpose was to
review offset proposals being negotiated by U.S. firms. In
1978, the Department of Defense decided to continue monitoring offset agreements, but not to have the United States
government involved in backing, negotiating, or satisfying
any U.S. company's offset commitment.

Faced with a higher offset commitment in its second F-5
sale, Northrop parceled out some of the obligation to its

main subcontractor, General Electric (GE), the engine supplier, on a prorated basis. The offset agreement included a potential 5 percent penalty on any unfulfilled portions of the offset commitment to be paid as a fine. Such an amount may not seem like much but could still cut significantly into a profit margin.

Kaelin indicated that this precedent-setting offset arrangement accomplished several Swiss objectives. Most important, it provided access and direct marketing assistance to new markets by committing the two prime contractors to export Swiss products internationally. In the case of the required Swiss machine tools, the offset agreement created an ironic situation where the U.S. company had to facilitate limited exports into the U.S. market, where U.S. machine tool companies were having a hard time making sales for a number of reasons not related to offsets. Eventually, both GE and Northrop set up trading companies to carry out the offset trading objectives.

Because of this F-5 offset agreement, a memorandum of understanding was signed in 1975 by the Swiss Defense Minister and Secretary of Defense James Schlesinger. This memorandum accomplished two vital further Swiss objectives: eliminating "buy American" restrictions; the other was a waiver of import duties. The Swiss even set up an office in their Washington embassy to advise their companies on how to win U.S. defense subcontracts. This breakthrough was hailed with a good deal of satisfaction by the Swiss. One official described the arrangement as "job-active" since the promotion of exports leads to new jobs in Switzerland. The offset is also clearly meant to enhance the Swiss defense industry by opening up more sales to it. Kaelin summed up the Swiss position directly and truthfully: "We use offset agreements as door openers to tear down 'buy American' restrictions. Without offset you don't get close to the foreign buyer."

The 1975 memorandum of understanding with Switzerland (supporting the offset concept of reciprocal procurement) set a pattern. Agreements were signed with the United Kingdom in 1975, with Turkey, Portugal, Norway, Italy, West Germany, France, Egypt, Denmark, and Belgium by 1980, and with Spain and Israel in 1983 and 1984, respectively.* These agreements were signed not for business reasons favorable to the United States, but for the security reason of accommodating our allies' need to develop their own defense industries. Another, more political purpose of the agreement was to relieve domestic pressure inside Europe regarding larger-than-ever military purchases from the United States. The agreements were proof to electorates and governments in Europe that the United States would be working harder to buy European products.

For better or worse, these memoranda helped to proliferate offset policies in Europe. By 1981, in the short span of six years, the offset system had become firmly established† (see Ref. 2, p. 8). No retreat seems likely. U.S. companies must continue to deal with the increasing burden of offset in ever more ingenious ways. It is useful to understand some of the agreements originating from individual countries, since they have mostly been signed with our important trading partners.

SWITZERLAND

The Swiss have followed up their first agreement with additional requests for offsets. In 1982, the Hughes Aircraft

---

*Similar agreements had been signed with Australia in 1973 and Canada in 1956.

†In 1982, when the United States government conducted one of its earliest surveys of offset obligations accepted by U.S. companies during 1975 to 1981, they recorded 143 contracts requiring offset. The total value of the contracts, many of which were defense-oriented, was $15.2 billion; the value of the associated offset commitments was $9.6 billion.

Company sold a $50 million Maverick missile system and agreed to an offset of 30 percent of the contract price for a term lasting until 1990. In January 1984, Litton Industries sold an inertial navigation system for about $10 million to Switzerland and accepted a 30 percent offset commitment lasting five years.

In 1984, the Swiss concluded a remarkable offset negotiation with West Germany to support their purchase of some 4 billion Swiss francs' worth of Leopard II tanks. The German manufacturer, Kraus-Maffei, proposed 100 percent offset with much of the manufacturing to be carried out under a licensee in Switzerland, with the remainder of the offset to be fulfilled through exports. Effectively, the Swiss were creating a new state-of-the-art tank industry that may one day surpass even the Leopard II. The competing U.S. tank, the M-1, lost out allegedly "not because of the offset but because orders could not be placed until 1986 and the tank had to be modified to meet Swiss specifications."

With no small amount of irony, one Swiss official summarized the offset situation by complaining about Pentagon restrictions on military purchases from Europe. "Let's go back to free trade," he said, while suggesting that a "buy Swiss act" ought to be enacted back home to counter the Pentagon's "buy American" policy.

THE UNITED KINGDOM

The United Kingdom has a military offset policy that has displeased some of its own officials. One complained that "American companies have never really lived up to their obligations. They live by the letter and not by the spirit of these agreements." The companies, of course, regard the offsets as a burden required by U.K. policy and their own need to make a sale.

An informal U.K. policy has evolved on a case-by-case basis, and there are certain unwritten rules. Offset is normally required only for significant purchases above $5 million in value. The degree and quality of the offset are determined by the competitive situation. "It is more difficult to extract an offset commitment from a company when there is no competition," said one official. "Military requirements" take precedence over domestic industrial and political concerns although these do play an important role.

Along with many other Europeans, the British feel that offsets at a most basic level respond to such issues by "providing jobs." More important, U.K. requirements stress that much of the offset should be in components made by the competing U.K. company that lost the sale. This policy of "like offsets" is sensitive to the security implications of undermining a domestic technology with a purchase from its competing foreign company. A British official justified overseas purchases in terms of the considerable start-up costs required to make strategic weapons: "While Britain's defense industry has great capacity, buying abroad in the strategic area saves money."

A supporting example of the "like offsets policy" was given regarding the U.K. purchase of a U.S. missile system. The sales agreement called for one-third of the missile's actual components to be built in the United Kingdom by the very companies that lost the sale. The rest of the 100 percent plus offset comprised items purchased in the area of defense high technology. General industrial goods or consumer products were excluded from the offset. In a similar competition for a Royal Navy sale, a U.K. official predicted that "the U.S. bidder closest to the 100 percent offset value requested would be most likely to win." This sort of bidding war policy infuriates U.S. and other companies.

The U.K. government insists that it carefully monitor these offset agreements to be sure that the cost of doing the offset (i.e., a trading company's commission) "is not put in the price." "We will not pay a premium for offset," a U.K. official said. In practice, of course, companies do everything to absorb the cost in the price; an offset can cause a successful bid to lose money if the cost of handling it turns out to be greater than expected.

The offset policy extends into the area of actively promoting the United Kingdom's own defense sales. The government has offered offsets to promote sales of the British Aerospace Company Rapier missile in a variety of countries. One such sale went, perhaps expectedly, to the Swiss. When Switzerland bought the antiaircraft missile system in 1981, it received a $50 million offset commitment, partly in licensed subcomponents and partly in general exports. The official observed that "some of our British companies arrogantly believe that British industry is competitive enough to win" most defense sales. In reality, he says government support is needed to give British industry a chance. The advantage of the British system is that such decisions to support a transaction can be taken "within the executive; no review process is necessary as in your Congress." "The real disadvantage to this system," said the official, is that "it's done in typical British government fashion; we make it up as we go along."

In late 1986, Boeing won a remarkable and hotly contested sale to the Royal Air Force of its AWACS (Airborne Warning and Control System), a 707 with a large radar dish and crammed internally with electronics, beating out further development of the United Kingdom's troubled Nimrod program. Boeing had originally intended to offer 35 percent offset, then raised it to 100 percent and, finally, to 130 percent. The program that evolved illustrates two important trends.

First, the percentage of offset attached to the sale is still rising, surpassing even the value of the sale itself. Second, by making the offset package larger and more complex, including long-term service and training agreements, Boeing created even more opportunity to make money. Boeing's competitors included not only U.K.'s General Electric, the Nimrod contractor, but other U.S. companies. Boeing won the sale by offering offset valued at 130 percent of the multibillion-dollar AWACS contract value. Three U.K. companies, Plessy, Racal Electronics, and Ferranti, actually supported Boeing's offer because they will receive numerous subcontracts under the arrangement in such areas as electronic warfare, systems integration, software, data communications, and simulation.

WEST GERMANY

A West German defense official compared the Federal Republic's offset policy to the United Kingdom's: "There are no standard regulations. Everything is on a case by case basis as done by the British Ministry of Defense." West German offset policy also parallels the United Kingdom's emphasizing not only jobs but maintaining with subcontracts a "high degree of technical sophistication within the local industry."

The Roland-for-Patriot missile transaction is a good case in point, having been cleared by the U.S. and German defense departments in July 1984.

In their purchase of over one billion dollars of Raytheon Patriot missiles from the United States, the West Germans negotiated an offset requiring the United States government to purchase Roland antiaircraft missiles *from* West Germany and to base them *in* West Germany. An additional $500 million offset is required of Raytheon to be placed through subcontracts in West Germany with AEG and Siemens. Imbalances can be adjusted with cash.

A similar arrangement occurred when Boeing sold NATO the AWACS airborne radar system in the late 1970s. As part of the offset, Boeing was required to purchase some AWACS components from Dornier, a large West German aircraft company.

Another West German and European technique to promote sales with an offset concept is to develop a joint venture as a way of selling the product to participating countries. This technique accomplishes virtually all of the objectives of an offset and has the added advantage of spreading the risk. Thus, the C-160 Transall transport plane is a joint venture between MBB and Aerospatiale, the giant French aerospace company, with initial sales going to West Germany and France.

The Panavia Company was similarly formed by West Germany, Italy, and the United Kingdom to manufacture the Tornado, a multi-role combat aircraft. Basically, the central fuselage is made by MBB at a plant near Munich; the tail section is made by the Italian firm, Aeritalia, in Turin; and the front section is made by British Aerospace in the United Kingdom. The group hopes that sales will be generated outside the funding partner companies, and indeed, the Saudis have already expressed an interest in buying a variation of the Tornado. The successful Airbus was similarly started as a joint venture among five European countries, which also agreed to purchase the first planes. Among U.S. companies, Boeing has pioneered this informal offset approach by purchasing some components for its 767 from Japan, one of the most important markets for the program.

Canada

PORTUGAL

Portugal developed an offset policy in the late 1970s with the purchase of five Lockheed L-1011 commercial jets. As in most countries requiring offset, its policy extends beyond the military into commercial aircraft.

Because the Portugese aircraft industry was not sufficiently developed to allow co-production, the Lockheed agreement called for the export of $59 million in Portugese products and services. This arrangement had to be approved by the government over a ten-year period. There are quotas of exports to be achieved at five-, seven-, and ten-year intervals. Penalty for noncompliance was to be paid in spare parts for the aircraft. A formal list of "primary target areas" for the offset was established including such items as aeronautical services and products, machine tools, textiles, telecommunications equipment, and automotive products. In this way, the offset helped to carry out an enhancement program of export stimulation for selected local industries.

More recently, the Portuguese have required a $10 million offset in defense-related products for the purchase of military trucks from DAF, a Dutch defense contractor. Portuguese officials have also discussed requiring offsets for the purchase of F-5 or F-20 aircraft from Northrop and appear likely to apply this policy to all aircraft purchases in either the defense or commercial areas. Portugal received an offset package of about 30 percent of contract value in the purchase of frigates from West Germany's Blohm & Voss.

CANADA

Canada has developed an aggressive offset program negotiated with defense contractors on a case-by-case basis. In both the 1985 OMB survey[2] and the one done in 1982, Canada was the country receiving the largest total dollar amount of offset commitments from U.S. companies. There are no set percentages in Canadian policy although these have generally tended to be high.

Usually there are penalties, although some contractors have persuaded the Canadians to agree on the performance of an offset on a "best efforts" basis. One peculiarity of the Canadian system is that extra credit is given for developing exports from a less-developed region of the country. The Canadian attaché justified his program, reflecting the kind of regionalism that has plagued Canadian politics: "After the offset program began to generate successes, the parts of the country that didn't benefit began to complain."

Another feature of the Canadian system is to promote informally a broad list of exports, including such diverse items as forest products and the development of tourist packages, in addition to awarding credit for more traditional defense electronics components. Using an offset policy, before purchasing some $3 billion of electronics for the ships of its navy, the Canadians insisted that Sperry set up a new subsidiary company in their country. The new electronics company, Paramax, was praised by a Canadian official as an "Adam's rib operation," emphasizing Canadian hopes of developing a whole electronics industry from Paramax.

McDonnell-Douglas offered a diverse offset package supporting its F-18 sale. The package included subcontracts related to the other aircraft programs outside the F-18 area as well as a proposal to promote tourism.

The Canadian government is pragmatic and aggressive in its use of offset and countertrade policy to facilitate industrial programs. It has required a large offset in the bidding for a ground radar system, and has arranged, through a partial barter, for the sale of a nuclear power plant to Rumania.

AUSTRALIA

An Australian offset program, called Industry Participation, is both the oldest program and one of the most successful in receiving commitments from U.S. companies. A U.S. embassy official based in Australia stated that by his count 80 percent of Australian offset obligations were held by U.S. companies. The Australian commercial attaché commented that his country's program favors a relatively stable offset percentage of 30 percent with a defined list of acceptable products, mostly in defense or related industries. Australia has also awarded offset credit for the purchase of New Zealand products. Well-known Australian exports such as wool, wheat, beef, and minerals are specifically excluded. The Australian government publishes a list of regional defense advisors who can refer U.S. and international contractors to capable local companies. The Australians also encourage co-production and technology transfer.

For example, McDonnell-Douglas is buying components in Australia to support the sale of its F-18. Similarly, Boeing co-produces ailerons in Australia to support the sale of 767 commercial aircraft to Quantas. IBM established a typewriter factory as part of a mainframe sale to the government.

FRANCE

The French, as always, appear to act differently by purchasing relatively small amounts of defense imports and, therefore, have perhaps fewer offset commitments from U.S. companies than the United Kingdom or West Germany. A French defense attaché summed up this policy: "France does not *buy* arms; it *sells* them!" However, the French may be catching up. For example, with a recent purchase of

AWACS from Boeing they extracted a 130 percent offset commitment from the Seattle-based company, equal to its recent prior sale in the United Kingdom. The French also created important background for offset by negotiating a memorandum of understanding with the United States similar to the one signed between the United States and Switzerland. The memorandum called for an overall balance of military sales between the two countries and eliminated duties and "buy American" provisions. It also puts pressure on the United States government to encourage arms purchases from France, and the French defense companies (e.g., Aerospatiale, Matra, and Dassault) are struggling mightily to build market share in the United States.

Informally, the French have emphasized a U.S. content policy in promoting Airbus sales to the United States. When the large 1984 sale to Pan Am was announced, Airbus Industries ran a two-page advertisement in *The Wall Street Journal* pointing out that five hundred U.S. subcontractors would benefit from the sale.

The largest of these subcontractors is, of course, General Electric, which makes the engines. It is interesting to note that the French have always insisted on French content within the GE engines sold to Airbus. In what appears to be another version of offset, the French raised that percentage (from about 25 percent) by getting GE to form a fifty-fifty joint venture with the French manufacturer, SNECMA, in order to win the engine contract for the new generation of Airbus (the A 320). The French do not always include U.S. content voluntarily, as in the Airbus example.

In two notable cases, French companies were actually required, by law, to include U.S. subcontractors when selling to the United States. For sales to the New York and San Francisco subway systems, the French manufacturer was required by *municipal* local content code (*not by U.S. foreign policy*) to include U.S. subcontractors. One such subcontractor was the important U.S. company, Westinghouse. It is ironic that the only formal offset requirement I have found imposed on a European importer is in these codes, not in Federal statutes. The policy has certainly been effective in assuring U.S. participation and could serve as a role model if our Federal authorities choose to adopt more offset codes.

OFFSET IN OTHER COUNTRIES

I collected numerous descriptions of offset transactions for Spain (see Chapter 5), Japan, Italy, Austria, Greece, Turkey, the Netherlands, Belgium, Denmark, Norway, Sweden, Finland, Israel, Egypt, South Korea, and Saudi Arabia. There are many similarities with the previous offset examples, including schemes for general exporting, co-production, investment, and technology transfer; centralized government staffs for negotiating and monitoring the agreements; and national policies that emphasize the domestic benefits of offset. Many European diplomats stressed the last point when speaking of offset as a necessary evil. "We don't even like the word 'countertrade,'" said a Norwegian official, "even though it is good for our companies." A Danish official explained: "We simply cannot afford these expensive programs without the participation of Danish workers." A Finnish official lamented: "As a policy we don't think this is the right way to develop international trade." A Dutch military attaché emphasized that large defense purchases "have got to be a two-way street." An Austrian official put it this way: "I don't think offset makes sense in Western countries. I would prefer competition based on price. But we need to tell our people who question defense spending that the money is coming back."

European countries not only developed individual offset policies, they often collaborated with one another to achieve an even more effective offset policy. In the F-16 program, Norway, Denmark, and Belgium agreed to let their partner, the Netherlands, assemble the planes, while they manufactured certain components and shipped them in for assembly. This was a reasonable solution because the planes had to be assembled in a central location. A Danish official commented that a similar approach is being used with Raytheon's Sea Sparrow. This missile system, first built for the U.S. Navy, is partially financed by a group of NATO countries. Although the missile is assembled at Raytheon, the NATO countries produce some components and are eventual buyers of the missile. Export sales to the allies outside this linked group are being promoted as well. Similarly, Japan has negotiated a co-production and technology transfer agreement with Raytheon to support its purchase of the Patriot missile.

Governments of Third World countries are also finding that when they negotiate with companies, they have a tremendous advantage. The slightest competition for a few large military purchases makes it a simple matter to demand offset. Turkey, Greece, and South Korea developed multi-billion-dollar offset programs when they purchased the F-16 from General Dynamics. Once a country experiences the economic benefits of offsets, and the political benefit of developing a patron–client relationship with major defense contractors in the United States or Europe, it is hard not to develop an ongoing offset program for other purchases as well. In the last few years, South Korea has developed formal offset guidelines and established an office in the Ministry of Defense to review proposals and supervise the programs. Offset is routinely requested now for all significant military purchases. Even Saudi Arabia, which once bought everything for cash before the fall in oil prices, is finding the offset path irresistible. In their major "peace shield" defense program, costing tens of billions of dollars, the Saudis have requested that all bids be accompanied by offset proposals to invest further in their country and to export Saudi products. They have, of course, received scores of proposals from the major defense companies of the world. Within the scope of this offset program, Boeing committed to build a Saudi aerospace industry valued at $500 million in order to win a large air-defense contract.

In the period of 1984–1987, Israel has been able to take advantage of a unique ruling by the U.S. Defense Department in its favor, permitting it to require 15 percent offsets of the total value for goods and services supplied under FMS credits. This ruling permitted Israel to collect $225 million of offset in fiscal year 1985. The program continued through 1986 and 1987 and then phased out. It is the only example where the United States government is still directly involved in offsets. For all offsets in the period 1980–1984, including those outside the FMS support, Israel's total of $1,477 million is exceeded only by Spain and Canada (see Table 3).

CONCLUSION

Military offsets are both a monster to be slain and an opportunity to be seized. The concept has spread since 1975 throughout Europe and now to Japan, Australia, Canada, and the larger trading countries in the Third World. Offset concepts are spreading to areas outside defense such as telecommunications. The value of offset packages has quickly increased, even surpassing the value of the contract value to which they are linked. U.S. companies are in no position to ask foreign governments to control or eliminate their requests for offset. That is the responsibility of the

Table 3   VALUE OF OFFSET OBLIGATIONS BY COUNTRY
(In millions of dollars)

COUNTRY	1980	1981	1982	1983	1984	TOTAL
Australia	20.8	1014.4	112.4	3.1	5.1	1156.7
Belgium	—	—	—	99.5	—	99.5
Canada	2714.6	34.6	—	—	61.4	2810.6
Denmark	8.2	—	1.1	4.5	0.8	14.6
Egypt	—	—	—	13.5	—	13.5
Greece	—	—	—	3.4	—	3.4
Israel	276.2	228.6	8.2	58.5	905.9	1477.4
NATO	291.6	—	—	—	—	291.6
Netherlands	3.2	702.0	12.0	—	280.3	997.5
New Zealand	1.2	—	—	—	—	1.2
Norway	10.8	3.1	—	14.9	42.4	71.2

Philippines	—	—	—	0.1	—	0.1
Singapore	—	—	—	45.0	—	45.0
South Korea	125.0	—	—	—	31.1	156.1
Spain	7.7	2.6	15.4	2334.0	44.3	2404.0
Sweden	—	570.0	—	33.7	—	603.7
Switzerland	158.0	30.0	—	4.0	—	192.0
Turkey	—	—	—	—	1071.0	1071.0
United Kingdom	—	—	—	17.8	206.2	224.0
Yugoslavia	—	—	—	5.7	—	5.7
France, Italy	—	54.0	—	—	—	54.0
Norway, Denmark	—	—	16.7	—	—	16.7
Belgium, Denmark, Norway,	—	—	—	—	—	—
Netherlands	29.1	17.0	11.2	14.3	274.9	346.6
TOTALS	3646.4	2656.4	181.1	2648.0	2924.1	12056.0

Courtesy: 1985 OMB Report on military offsets.

United States government. From the U.S. corporation's viewpoint, offset is a problem to be lived with, creating opportunities as well as headaches for skillful dealmakers.

Devising offset transactions requires a form of relational thinking that is very similar to the concept of joint-venturing and even subcontracting. One major goal of European offset policy is to create opportunities for domestic companies to share in sales and technology. Larger companies, like Boeing, are finding that offset agreements are a way of expanding the scope of a transaction, creating more opportunities for profit. What they give up in subcontracts and co-production, they more than recover in service agreements, training, and ultimately building market position in a country over time.

The challenge of offset is that its complexity gives a skillful company many ways to build a relationship with the host country.

The danger is that offsets also create more risk of problems of noncompliance, poor service, and misunderstanding. The competitive forces that favor the rise of offsets can make it difficult in these cases to win future sales in a country.

At the same time, the United States government must recognize that it is partly to blame for creating the offset situation by signing the series of reciprocal procurement memoranda discussed above. There was a time when these agreements may have been necessary for the legitimate U.S. security concern of accommodating our allies' domestic economic and political needs. In light of the recent huge U.S. trade deficits, it may be time to develop other approaches that emphasize both national security and economics.

One approach would be for the U.S. Defense Department to consider purchasing some selected European weapons or other nonstrategic military items, while attaching as a condition offset requirements to benefit certain U.S. industries. This would accommodate a long-standing European frustration with being able to sell few defense items to the Pentagon. A kind of pseudo-offset policy has been in effect for some time for Pentagon procurement. The Department of Defense does not buy foreign equipment unless there is an agreement that it is totally fabricated in the United States. This "buy American" policy is designed to assure the Defense Department access to military supplies regardless of whether a foreign source goes neutral or is overrun. The policy exasperates our NATO allies, who might see the benefits of a link between a new offset policy that increases Pentagon purchases from overseas and European commitments to buy more from the United States.

Another approach is for the United States government to begin identifying various segments of offset, such as missiles or military aircraft, as subjects for negotiations. Some hard bargaining through the General Agreement on Tariffs and Trade (GATT) and directly with European governments is badly needed to curb their growing appetite for offsets.

We may find that, like foreign subsidized export credits, we cannot negotiate offset away and may be lucky to hold it in check. It would be difficult to go to the bargaining table, however, if we are not prepared to develop a tough offset policy of our own. If our experience parallels that of the European allies, we may find real benefits from offsets beyond their being mere bargaining chips.

Chapter Five

Grassfire in Spain: Creating a National Offsets Policy

"The name of the game is offset."
—Commercial Attaché, U.S. Embassy in Madrid

• 71 •

SPAIN ADOPTS OFFSET

As was made clear in Chapter 4, military offsets appear to have begun in earnest in 1975 when Switzerland purchased Northrop's F-5 and the NATO countries (the Netherlands, Belgium, Denmark, and Norway) bought the F-16. Interest in offsets spread quickly throughout Europe and the Third World. Spain appears to have gone into offset business relatively late, after 1980. The rapid development of offset policy in Spain says something about the appeal of offsets to foreign governments and their effectiveness in getting importers to comply.

In an unclassified cable back to the State Department, commercial attaché John Perkins was making an important observation about the recent Spanish development of an offset policy: "The name of the game is offset. Generally speaking, all significant government purchases—aerospace, telecommunications, whatever—now appear to have an offset component or a local content requirement."

Michael Cosgrove, vice president of Countertrade and Barter at General Electric (GE), confirmed this view: "Spain has become one of the shrewdest countries in requesting offset. They have become very knowledgeable very quickly."

A survey carried out by the U.S. Office of Management and Budget reinforces this point. U.S. companies signed offset obligations with Spain of $7.7 million in 1982, $2,334 million in 1983, and $44.3 million in 1984. In less than five years, Spain has gone from requiring virtually no offsets before 1980 to requiring them on practically every major purchase from overseas by 1985. For example, as part of a telecommunications offset, AT&T is co-investing with the Spanish national phone company to build a factory in Spain that will assemble and sell components to the Spanish telephone system. The U.S. embassy also observed that the amount of offset required for each sale appears to be rising. In 1985, the 30 percent of contract value that had once been an upper target became the minimally accepted floor, with many transactions higher than that.

RISE IN OFFSETS

The huge 1983 rise in offset was caused by McDonnell-Douglas's sale of 72 F-18 fighter aircraft to Spain. As happened in Turkey and Korea with the major F-16 sales, a single large military purchase caused the government to begin creating a national countertrade policy.

The McDonnell-Douglas offset requirement was for over $2 billion, 100 percent of the sales price. As reported by the U.S. embassy, there are several features characteristic of other large offset agreements, including both direct and indirect offsets, technology transfer, and supporting roles in the offset played by the leading subcontractors, Northrop and GE. Included in the offset are several hundred million dollars in co-production of the F-18s by Construcciónes Aeronauticas (Casa), the Spanish aircraft manufacturer, and by several Spanish subcontractors including Aisa and Marconi Española for such items as ground flight simulators. McDonnell-Douglas is also committed to generating $1.8 billion in additional Spanish exports, new investments, and tourism receipts.

To fulfill such a large commitment, McDonnell-Douglas has worked hard to qualify local manufacturers for participation in the F-18 program and to advise others of new export opportunities. The St. Louis-based firm carried out marketing surveys and screening of Spanish products, including surveys of both Spanish and U.S. investors, and had discussions with Spanish companies and the government about needed technology transfers. The U.S. embassy has been helpful by identifying companies in the small Spanish aerospace industry wishing to export. It reported, for example, 30 companies identified by a Spanish commission with the ability to participate in the Strategic Defense Initiative (SDI).

MAJOR OBJECTIVES

The major objective of Spanish offset policy is to develop a national defense capability, both to foster its own self-reliance and to develop an export capability in this lucrative business. The Ministry of Defense in November 1985 published a policy on offsets, listing as goals:

(1) full Spanish defense industry participation in multi-national projects and national projects;

(2) improving the technological level of Spanish industry; and

(3) fostering national economic, commercial, and labor interests.

The policy emphasized not only building technology and production, but also weapons systems maintenance. Like many national offset policies, it called for a detailed description of any offset proposed by a U.S. company, a list of Spanish exporters to participate, dates for carrying out the program, and performance guarantees or penalties for non-performance. As an example of its sensitivity to an over-reliance on the United States, Spain declined to buy an additional 72 F-18s to meet the established requirement for 144. Instead, the Spanish plan to develop through Casa a two-engine, subsonic attack plane with advanced electronics and heavy load capability to replace the F-18 in the interdiction and ground support role, freeing the more expensive F-18 for air superiority, deep penetration, and long-range patrol missions.

U.S. manufacturers must cope also with Spain's desire to seek closer relations with European countries by the awarding of a defense contract. Such a geopolitical consideration may have played a role in Spain's recent decision not to buy an air missile defense system (the Chaparral) from Ford Aerospace, but to buy the Roland system instead from its French neighbor, Aerospatiale.

IMPACT ON U.S. COMPANIES

A major impact of the offset policy on U.S. companies has been to make competition for sales in Spain much tougher. For example, Westinghouse declined to bid on an air traffic control primary radar because the offset requirements were considered too high. Instead, the bid was won by a Spanish company in collaboration with Marconi of Great Britain. Enterprise Electronics of the United States offered to participate in a co-investment scheme with the Spanish company, Cecelsa, but still failed to win a tender for a civilian meteorological system.

According to the U.S. embassy, the Spanish Ministry of Defense is requesting ever greater amounts of offset. A bureaucracy to review and administer the offset programs in the Ministry of Defense has been built up since 1985. Requests for technology transfer have increased, and the accounting for offsets is tougher. The offset concept has spread beyond defense to other commercial sectors. In telecommunications sales, the vendor must guarantee that local firms are trained to carry out maintenance functions. In the area of commercial aircraft, Boeing has an arrangement with Casa for the co-production of components in the 767s sold to Iberia, Spain's national airline. The European Airbus has a similar arrangement with Casa for the Airbus aircraft sold to Iberia. Casa appears to have been a prime beneficiary of the offset program, but other local firms have been lined up to co-produce everything from computer consoles for the Lamps antisubmarine system to guidance electronics and propulsion motors for missiles and turrets for tank systems.

A final complication for U.S. companies wishing to sell in Spain may be an apparent United States government agreement with Spain pledging to seek an "equitable balance" in defense and other areas of trade, creating an issue at the heart of Spain's offset policy. On the surface, such commitments, which are made to other allies as well, appear to be fair and reasonable. It is only natural, from a security point of view, that the United States would want to accommodate its valuable NATO ally's need to foster the growth of its own defense industry.

However, such a concept of trade balancing indirectly encourages Spain to promote offsets and poses a real challenge to U.S. companies seeking to make sales. A policy motivated by U.S. security considerations does not take into account business and commercial implications. In a country such as Spain where the United States is very effective in selling defense equipment, the United States is pledging through bilateral trade balancing clauses to encourage U.S. companies to transfer technology, to co-produce, and to export, or to risk losing significant sales.

CONCLUSION

Reconciling security or foreign policy goals with the commercial goal of making export sales is a particularly difficult problem for the United States in its role as a principal defender of the free world. Spain is one of the better examples of our dilemma. If we are going to pledge to seek a commercial balance in Spain where we have had a lot of success in exporting, we must work even harder to achieve balancing with countries where we are not so successful, such as Japan.

Chapter Six

Spectacular Dealmaking
with Oil Barter

"Oil-based barter could not have begun
before the oil price increases in the early 1970s."
—U.S. State Department Specialist

It can be argued that the proliferation of countertrade beyond central Europe is in large part due to the oil price increase after 1973. Military offsets in Europe were devised to keep scarce hard currency at home, available ultimately to pay sharply increased oil bills. Debt crises brought on by oil in Third World countries similarly proved fertile ground during the 1970s and 1980s for countertrade transactions, especially in Latin America and Africa.

WHY OIL BARTER?

A reasonable person might ask, With money pouring into Middle Eastern coffers, why should there be any oil barter at all? In 1984 one State Department analyst suggested that actually the softening of the oil price in the early 1980s caused oil barter to accelerate to an estimated 15 percent of world oil trading. It was a way of discounting to deal with the soft oil prices, enabling the purchaser to get more value by trading oil for product than by selling it for cash at a steep discount. Barter also solved a political problem by giving Organization of Petroleum Exporting Countries (OPEC) nations and other producers a way around official OPEC price ceilings. In addition, it was a way around production quotas, and it may have provided commissions to powerful people in oil-producing countries.

A Westinghouse trading officer observed that oil barter transactions were among the most difficult to put together because of price volatility and problems with availability. In scores of countertrade deals put together by Westinghouse, he had seen only two proposed oil barter transactions. One did not work out because the purchaser decided to pay cash. In the other a South American country was not able to supply the oil it promised.

LARGE-SCALE TRANSACTIONS

Despite such difficulties, oil barter transactions are among the most spectacular and include some of the largest countertrade transactions ever.

In 1985, Saudi Arabia tried very hard to purchase $4 billion worth of fighter jets and jet trainers from U.S. companies. Because of soft oil prices and the difficulty in mobilizing cash quickly, the Saudis proposed to pay some 60 percent of the purchase price with oil. The United States government, which of course must approve such defense exports, decided to oppose this transaction because it did not want U.S. companies accepting oil as payment, and relations with Israel made such a large arms shipment to Saudi Arabia sensitive. Prime Minister Thatcher lobbied hard to win this sale for the United Kingdom. It was suggested at the time by some competitors that she called President Reagan to verify his position against the sale and to be certain the United States government would not be offended if the United Kingdom won the deal by accepting Saudi oil. British Aerospace did eventually win this valuable contract. The transaction came back to haunt the U.S. defense industry because in 1988, as a follow-up sale, Saudi Arabia agreed to purchase from the United Kingdom additional fighter aircraft, other defense equipment, and base development services, valued at over $10 billion. In the initial 1985 sale, there was some serious heartburn at British Aerospace when oil prices dropped further after the sale, but the corporation had covered itself well enough to claim that it still got an excellent deal.

The best way for a manufacturing company to protect itself from such price fluctuations is to let a trading company handle the oil as well as most of the trading risk. In 1984, Boeing reportedly brought in the Japanese trading company

C. Itoh and several other trading companies to handle the large quantities of oil it received for a commercial fleet of Boeing 747s. This oil swap was valued at over $1 billion. The details of this remarkable transaction have not been released to the public. As the leader of OPEC, the Saudis are understandably sensitive to speculation about the use of countertrade as a way to deviate from oil prices established by the cartel. In the Boeing sale, foreign exchange generated from the sale was left in interest-bearing accounts long enough to bring overall cash levels up to OPEC price guidelines.

The French company, SCOA International, completed an oil barter and escrow financing arrangement with Nigeria, carefully conditioned against oil price fluctuation. The transaction, which involved an exchange of oil for Peugeot knock-down automobile kits, included a phase-out clause linked to a fall in oil prices (see Ref. 5, p. 41). When prices did fall, the transaction was terminated in 1985 after about $200 million in trade had taken place.

NATIONAL INTEREST

Bartering oil not only gives a country access to goods at discount prices, but more important still, it makes it possible to accomplish high priority objectives in the national interest.

National Security

One such reason for bartering oil is for national security purposes, a rationale applying to both Iran and Iraq during the brutal and costly war fought between 1980 and 1988. As oil prices softened, it became crucial for them to get maximum value for their crude. Beginning in 1981, Volvo of

Sweden sold $250 million of buses to Iran for bartered oil, largely because Volvo agreed to calculate the oil value at official OPEC prices, higher than the more realistic Rotterdam spot market. Volvo adjusted the number of buses on board against the value of oil in the Iranian tanker. One freighter with the correct value of buses was shipped against one oil tanker in each transaction. The two ships crossed in the ocean. As they struggled during wartime conditions to complete refining facilities at Bandar Khomeini and other strategic areas of Iran, Mitsubishi and other Japanese firms similarly accepted crude oil for at least partial payment. Iraq also exchanged its oil for manufactured goods as the oil prices collapsed in the mid-1980s, trading it for Volkswagens assembled at the huge plant outside São Paulo in Brazil.

There are reports too that Iraq linked some of its oil sales to the purchase of weapons from France, including Super Etendard fighters and Exocet missiles. One Iraqi official put the military need in understated terms: "Before the war, we didn't touch countertrade; during the war we were more receptive." Other countries that have bartered oil for weapons include Libya, which paid for some of its arms shipments from the Soviet Union through this method.

Reducing Debt

Another high priority reason to barter oil is to gain leverage in reducing external debt. The revenue from oil and gas increases in the 1970s was used by several OPEC nations (notably Libya, Algeria, and Nigeria) to service massive loans obtained to finance rapid industrialization programs. The fall of oil prices brought on a credit crunch as bank reserves dwindled and borrowing capacity was reduced. These countries are selectively bartering oil either to reduce debt directly or to avoid going to banks that are reluctant to finance new debt.

Italy negotiated a government-to-government oil barter with Libya in 1983 as a means of reducing by $1 billion the debt owed to Italian companies. Italy gave Libya a 10 percent discount on the debts (effectively forgiving 10 percent of the debt) and also agreed to accept the oil at the official OPEC price. One Italian official estimated that 10 percent of his country's trade with Libya and Algeria is now on the basis of oil barter. Turkish officials have also accepted Libyan oil as payment for debts to their country.

Buying Food and Equipment

Much of oil barter is aimed at the very basic purpose of buying food and equipment. An Algerian official stated that his country uses oil or LPG (liquefied petroleum gas) extensively to barter for machinery and equipment from Europe and other African countries. Algeria has also bartered for wheat from companies in the United States. Since the 1970s, Nigeria has traded oil to Brazil for agricultural commodities. Interestingly, this type of transaction was one of the early oil barter sales. Brazil, with its wealth of commodities, introduced the concept when it did not have the cash to pay for its much higher oil bill as prices first increased. In a 1980 transaction, despite the existence of a law on the books against oil barter, Venezuela traded oil to Brazil for commodities such as sugar. Mexico appears to be one of the few oil-producing countries not to have bartered its oil for food. An explanation for this could be its increased role in exporting to the United States, where companies have paid cash.

Avoiding Trading Difficulties

I suspect that some oil barter is for the convenience of avoiding trading commissions and other logistical difficulties in turning oil into cash. In 1983, the Kuwait Petroleum Corporation paid crude oil to a major U.S. company for its European oil refinery and lube oil plants. Volvo may have had such savings and tactical issues in mind as a motive for actually entering the oil business. In the early 1980s, the company bought a 30 percent interest in Hamilton Brothers Oil in Denver. Volvo also purchased the Beijer Group in Sweden, retaining its oil and food trading divisions while spinning off the rest. The company is now well positioned to transact countertrading in support of its significant truck, bus, and car sales to the Third World.

Oil is such a valuable commodity that it has been the object of perhaps more clever countertrading schemes than other commodities such as sugar or coffee. About 1980, for example, Brazil swapped its interest in the Majnoon oil field in eastern Iraq in return for a long-term oil-purchasing agreement. The war between Iran and Iraq, when several battles were fought through the swamps of Majnoon, no doubt impeded the oil flow in this transaction. Brazil also devised a scheme, called compensation, to refine Nigerian crude and to accept payment for this service in finished product. Ecuador has similarly bartered crude oil to Brazil and Venezuela to obtain gasoline for its own consumption.

NATURAL GAS

Natural gas is becoming, like oil, a commodity subject to clever countertrading among nations. The natural gas pipeline from the Soviet Union to Western Europe is being facilitated by countertrade, particularly concerning the selection of construction companies to be awarded building contracts for the pipeline. There is sure logic to a country's position that if it is to pay billions of dollars for gas, it wants local companies to receive a major share of the construction work. Such an issue held up for months a 27-year, $40 billion gas pipeline project between Norway's Statoil and Gaz de France. France insisted that French construction companies should be awarded most of the work and got its way when the transaction was recently closed. This policy is interesting because France has often sought to stay out of countertrade at government level. However, as one official said, when an objective is targeted as a major priority, "Orders come down to structure deals."[5] In both gas and oil transactions few countries have been able to resist this temptation, even at the highest levels of government, to demand a countertrade concession when the national interest is at stake.

SUMMARY

The oil price increases in the 1970s caused a few nations, such as Brazil, to use their wealth of commodities to countertrade for oil. When oil prices softened in the 1980s, the equation turned around. Oil producers began to barter their oil as a way of getting greater values and better prices. Like coffee and grains, oil is a commodity where the existence of a strong secondary market makes it more attractive for countertrade than manufactured goods. Commodities, in general, benefit from having a cadre of professional traders to facilitate the process with hedging in the futures market. Minerals and raw materials have some of the same characteristics also, and it should come as no surprise that Africa has seen its fair share of countertrade in these areas.

Chapter Seven

Solving Currency Problems in Africa

"This is one of the rare times when we just flat whipped our French competitor Harris after they had already been declared the winner."
—Official at Rockwell Trading Company
about a sale in Zimbabwe won through countertrade

The African continent, which has nurtured the earliest ancestors of mankind, has a mixed reputation as a place to do business. Africa's reputation is buffeted between images of a poverty-stricken sahel with little money to spend on imports and of Nigeria's capital, Lagos—overflowing with oil money and requests for baksheesh (pay to expedite service). On the contrary, many foreign companies have enjoyed profitable business relationships in Africa, whether in a peaceful, well-managed country like Senegal, oil-rich Gabon and Cameroons, or mineral-rich Ivory Coast, Zaire, or Zimbabwe. Natural resources have provided fertile ground for countertrade, which has begun to resolve a few currency problems and has provided the competitive edge for certain bids.

ZIMBABWE–ROCKWELL PRINTING PRESS SALE

The Zimbabwe–Rockwell printing press sale illustrates both the need for competitive financing and the miracle of resurrection that is occasionally possible through a skillfully structured countertrade. It was, as Pat Hall of Rockwell ruefully explained, one of those deals that had died. In 1983, a French company had already been declared the winner of the $8 million contract, thanks in large measure to favorable export financing that was heavily subsidized by the French government. The French loan was close to being a grant, no down payment was required, and there was 4 percent interest with a 20-year term. To get the best financing, since the U.S. Eximbank had become less active and adequate financing was not available, Rockwell sourced the transaction (i.e., built the printing press) through its British subsidiary in order to have an ECGD loan behind the transaction. (ECGD is the U.K. counterpart of the U.S. Eximbank.) Still this was not enough to win the sale. At the last moment, Rockwell proposed 100 percent countertrade in ferrochrome and nickel, knowing that Zimbabwe had an oversupply. A trading company was brought in to trade the metal. Since the contract was technically not yet signed with the French company, the award was changed to Rockwell. Pat explained that at the time his countertrade group was "euphoric, thinking we had found a key to winning every deal. The real world of course was consistently very tough in our bidding later on, but we had at least found one measure that could work in a desperate situation."

COUNTERTRADE IN AFRICA

Countertrade is often used in Africa to resolve a problem when everything else has failed. Because the economies of African countries are mostly small, the transactions tend to be small and are often structured around a barter approach. Major offset transactions are rare. The 1985 OMB study lists only $13.5 million in defense-related offset for Egypt among all countries on the African continent[2] (see Table 3). The nearest to an official countertrade policy at the governmental level appears to exist mainly in Egypt, South Africa, and Zimbabwe, although other countries have expressed interest in the process of formalizing and developing policy.

Zimbabwe

Zimbabwe recently introduced legislation concerning countertrade, setting guidelines for a newly formed review committee. In addition to approvals needed by the central bank and the grain board (where relevant), guarantees must be offered that reciprocal goods do not displace cash transactions, prices must be at market level, and the negotiated value of the trade goods must be disclosed. The guidelines are intended to supplement the current policy of limiting countertrade to priority imports, to penetrating new markets, or to disposing of excess production (see Ref. 5, p. 9). Ultimately, the willingness of an African country to countertrade depends on the current state of its commodity trading and the relative supply of the commodity in the country.

Zambia

A U.S. minerals company had a blocked currency* problem in Zambia and was able to resolve it thanks to a policy exception made on countertrade. The company benefited from a successful long-term business relationship with the country that made it easier to ask a favor. Permission was finally obtained from the Zambian central bank to use the blocked local currency to buy export minerals. Zambia had been reluctant to barter its valuable metals such as cobalt, copper, and uranium but did so in this case largely because of the diligence of one trader who made several trips to the country to structure the transaction.

Kenya

The movie *Sheena* was produced in Kenya with the blocked currency of Pepsico, Inc., the maker of Pepsi Cola and other soft drinks. Most of the actors were hired with the blocked local currency, except for the starlet who played Sheena.

---

*A blocked currency is one that is forbidden by government policy to be exchanged for hard currency and taken out of the country.

Fortunately, Sheena was a beautiful lady wearing a leather g-string and leading the forces of good across East Africa while riding bareback on a horse painted to look like a zebra. Although the critics panned the movie, its returns at the box office, in video, and from TV reruns have earned green dollars for its producers, and it is certainly one of the most creative countertrades ever attempted.

SWAPPING

If there is a typical transaction in Africa, it is likely to be a swap of some commodity for manufactured goods; these transactions span quite a spectrum.

The Democratic Republic of Madagascar (also known as the Malagashy Republic) used cloves, its major commodity, to resolve a pressing cash problem. A fertilizer factory was under construction and nearing completion. The government ran out of cash from the loan proceeds and could not pay the construction company, N-Ren International, a Brussels-based firm. A team was put in place to maintain the nearly completed plant. Finally, the government offered the contractor cloves. Despairing of ever being paid at all to complete the plant, the construction company accepted and took on the responsibility of selling cloves in the European market. The details of this transaction, emphasizing both problems and opportunities in structuring a barter transaction, are discussed in Chapter 8.

Egyptian government officials described transactions with Sudan in which medicine, chemicals, buses, and cars were traded for leather, livestock, ground nuts, and spices. In 1983, the Sudanese swapped watermelon seeds for Egyptian textiles. Officials of the two countries describe a formal adjustment process that takes place each year as the countries seek to balance more equitably this overall trading.

In Somalia, a European automaker traded buses and trucks for bananas and other agricultural products. A Kenya-based automotive company has bartered agricultural commodities for spare parts. Kenya has also tried, mostly unsuccessfully, to barter its stockpiles of pyrethrum (used in insecticides) and flourspar (used in cement).

Countertrades in other regions of Africa have emphasized mineral resources. Zaire negotiated with a European trading company to barter copper for a telecommunications system. The country has encouraged barter sales selectively, such as a cobalt-for-buses swap made in the early 1980s. Both the Ministry of Finance and the state mining company, Geacamines, must approve such transactions.

Several companies are negotiating with Guinea to use its valuable bauxite in countertrading. Ghana has traded salt for cattle with Upper Volta. An official pointed out a special problem in Ghana: "The country is rich in cocoa, timber, and gold ore and would like to countertrade more of these items. However, the local infrastructure has deteriorated so much in recent years that roads and trucks are not adequate for transporting the available exports to port." In Ghana, most observers agree there has been a real delivery problem to support countertrading. The lack of a convertible currency in Ghana means that consumer products are frequently available only on the black market for high markups.

In this sense the former French colonies have benefited over their U.K. counterparts in Africa. Most still have currencies tied to the value of the French franc, giving more stability and perhaps a little more value to their currencies. The former French colonies have also tended to have better managed economies.

In the late 1970s, Morocco, one of the African countries with special ties to France, traded phosphate from its huge reserves to the Soviet Union for oil and manufactured equipment. This success has caused the Moroccan government to become more supportive, encouraging countertrade when it can facilitate national priorities. According to a Moroccan official, the government has "pushed the private sector to countertrade when necessary."

South Africa is another resource-rich country that has countertraded, often because of its political and economic isolation. In 1982, South Africa traded minerals to Rumania for maize. The South African government, according to one official, is continuing to rethink its policy in a more supportive light. He declined for security reasons to say whether South Africa had swapped minerals for oil.

The most active countertrading countries in Africa appear to be Egypt and Nigeria. The latter has figured in a number of oil barter transactions, mentioned previously, but curiously maintains through its representation in Washington, D.C., a rather negative or ambivalent view toward the practice. Nigeria hopes to sell more oil for badly needed cash to repay the huge national debt run up during the oil boom days. A Nigerian official said his country is trying to encourage joint ventures or investments where the outsider investor is paid back in product, a practice called compensation.

This compensation concept, which has been extremely popular in the People's Republic of China, was used in Egypt for the development of a turnkey aluminum plant. The major Swiss company, Aluswiss, exports alumina to the plant and takes back a portion of the finished aluminum as payment for the investment. Yearly protocol agreements between Egypt and the Soviet Union and Eastern Bloc countries are still in existence, although some of these (e.g., with Hungary and Bulgaria) have been canceled since relations with the

Soviets deteriorated under President Sadat. Egypt trades limited amounts of petroleum, cotton, and chemicals in these transactions and receives wood products and consumer goods in return.

There is a real desire in Africa for countertrade proposals that offer investment and for proposals from corporations that emphasize good relations over the years. Frequently, when key government approvals are needed to make a transaction work, companies with strong relationships in an African country have been the most successful. This certainly seems to be true of the N-Ren barter transaction described in Chapter 8.

SUMMARY

Countertrade in Africa is characterized by certain patterns. Transactions are smaller, reflecting smaller scale economies. Offsets are virtually nonexistent. Formal, national countertrade policies like those existing in so many Latin American countries are not prevalent. When countertrade is used in Africa, it is often based on minerals or commodities because of the continent's rich natural resources. Barter-type transactions have helped to resolve some currency conversion problems or blocked currencies. Counterpurchase has been effective in giving a competitive edge to a bid or in generating the foreign exchange used by a country to purchase an import.

Chapter Eight

Saved by Cloves

*"The vessel with our shipment of cloves didn't show up on time.
It just disappeared. I finally tracked it down in a small
port on the Atlantic north of Lisbon, Portugal."*
—DON HART, partner with Guilfoil, Petzall and Shoemake of St. Louis, formerly
General Counsel of N-Ren International

*"I spent a week in Rotterdam trying to get the
ship's captain to stop unloading the cloves in the rain.
There was a lot of damage."*
—MILTON BROWN, senior trader with CMS Trading of Washington, D.C.,
formerly Director of Shipping and Insurance of N-Ren International

COMMERCIAL COUNTERTRADE

The recent series of barter transactions between N-Ren International (N-Ren) and the Democratic Republic of Madagascar (referred to here as Madagascar) is a classic example of commercial countertrade. This remarkable transaction illustrates a basic principle of countertrade. If a buyer wants to purchase something badly enough from a seller, and the buyer owns something of value, a way can be found to structure the transaction. Countertrade in this situation was a desperate, even heroic measure of last resort. However, it was far preferable to the cost of not having the fertilizer plant brought to completion. The transaction also suggests how countertrade need not be the special preserve of the large, multinational company or the huge defense contractor.

N-REN INTERNATIONAL

N-Ren International, a small engineering and construction firm based in Brussels, has put together fertilizer plants in a number of Third World countries. It began construction on a $60 million fertilizer plant in 1979 for Madagascar. By 1983, delays resulting in cost overruns caused the project to be put on hold.

N-Ren had fallen on hard times, sharing the misfortune of the fertilizer industry in particular, along with large engineering and construction firms in general. All faced drastic declines in business following the collapse in oil prices and the recession in the early 1980s.

In better times N-Ren built fertilizer factories in some of the less credit-worthy countries of Africa and South America. It had a good reputation as a place where adventurous young engineers and business school graduates could gain invaluable experience in international business. A former president, Cordell Hull, went on to a brilliant career at Bechtel, Inc. in San Francisco, serving as chief financial officer and then executive vice president for the corporation. He became one of the most influential officers in the company outside of the Bechtel family itself. N-Ren's current president, the American businessman, Thomas Snyder, presided over important successes with the completion of plants in Mauritius, Venezuela, and Burma, as well as the partial completion of contracts in Sudan and Madagascar. N-Ren's executive offices were based in a beautiful chateau in the village of Peutie in the suburbs of Brussels. The engineers worked in an attractive modern building recently constructed behind the chateau, which also had a magnificent restored Flemish guest house.

PROBLEMS IN MADAGASCAR

In these beautiful surroundings, Thomas Snyder wrestled with a business nightmare. Madagascar ran out of money to pay for N-Ren's fertilizer plant even as it neared completion. The country had fallen on hard times and its finances were tightly controlled under an International Monetary Fund (IMF) restructuring. The plant was about 95 percent completed by 1983, and 98 percent of the equipment was delivered to the factory site. Cost-escalation clauses would raise the price in future years well above the initial $60 million. The project, consisting of two plants, was located outside the port of Tamatave, near the only oil refinery in the country. The factory converted naptha feedstock into ammonia and then made urea fertilizer from ammonia at the rate of 1.74 tons of urea for every one ton of ammonia. Voest Alpine of Austria supplied the equipment for the ammonia plant,

Dominion Bridge of Canada the urea plant, and Ferrostaal of West Germany the offsites. The two plants together could produce 270 metric tons of fertilizer per day. Operating about 330 days per year, the combined plants could produce about 90,000 tons annually when running at full capacity.

Problems began when construction delays forced cost overruns. The initial financing, secured by the three equipment suppliers (Voest Alpine, Dominion Bridge, and Ferrostaal), could no longer cover the cost of the project. Madagascar was not able to meet its requirements for putting equity into the project. In the worldwide recession, the creditworthiness of Madagascar diminished, making new borrowing impossible. The hard currency in the central bank was targeted elsewhere to cover national debt. Both N-Ren and the government were concerned that inadequate funding would cause the nearly completed plant to be maintained inadequately. N-Ren kept a skeleton staff in place on a low budget with precious remaining funds, while negotiations proceeded on the cost overrun and equity financing problems. Snyder personally traveled to Tananarive, the capital of Madagascar, several times, trying to resolve the impasse— all to no avail. Finally, when the situation seemed hopeless, a breakthrough occurred. The government of Madagascar proposed to generate a cash flow for the project over several years by providing N-Ren with a spice for which the country is famous, cloves. Snyder's perseverance produced results.

CLOVES TO THE RESCUE

Cloves, along with vanilla beans, are Madagascar's critical exports, earning valuable foreign exchange, so this decision, years in the making, did not come about lightly. Both the Ministers of Finance and Agriculture gave their approval.

The Revolutionary Council, equivalent to the U.S. Cabinet, had to give its approval, and the personal consent of President Didier Ransiraka was needed also.

Fortunately for this barter transaction, Madagascar's government carefully controls the cloves industry, buying the spice directly from about 12 major private-sector growers on the island with local currency, the Malgache franc. This meant the government had easy, natural access to a commodity, a key requirement for countertrade. The suppliers accept local currency for their crops, not only because of a government decree, but because the Malgache franc is tied to the French franc, giving a more stable value than if left to float downward in inverse proportion to inflation.

In countries such as Turkey where the private sector is stronger and more developed than in Madagascar, the government can have a more difficult time in gaining access to the commodities necessary to barter, even when willing to undertake a transaction of this nature.

To develop the shipping and insurance commitments for the barter, Snyder chose Milton Brown, an officer with considerable experience in trading. Prior to joining N-Ren in 1972, Brown worked 20 years for Bunge, the large global grain trading company based in Argentina and Brazil. N-Ren's general counsel, Don Hart, served as legal troubleshooter for the transaction, supervised the financial arrangements, and reviewed the huge amount of documentation required. Snyder himself negotiated the contract for each barter shipment and structured the deal conceptually.

The first shipment of approximately 1,200 tons of cloves was scheduled for October 1983 with the ship arriving at Rotterdam in January 1984. The shipping agent in Hamburg, West Germany identified an available ship and facilitated contractual arrangements. Loss insurance was commissioned with a group organized by Lloyd's of London through a local insurer based in Liège, Belgium. The cloves were brought by the government to the port of Tamatave, coincidentally the site of the fertilizer plant. The general manager of the plant (a joint venture investment between N-Ren and the government) was present at dockside to inspect every 50-kilo bag loaded on board, "to be sure each contained cloves and not bricks," according to Hart. The bags were carefully examined by a number of inspectors for such parameters as weight, quality, condition, and possible contamination. The bags in the first shipment were of a quality called C-G3, a standard French measurement for cloves, meaning Charles George 3. When different qualities are shipped, the bags must be kept separate since each grower has his own marking, and there are slight potential differences in quality. For each 50-kilo bag, there were about eight to ten documents, including certificates of origin, weight, and quality, a certificate from Surveillance Générale Suisse (SGS) of Switzerland, a certificate of control and conditioning, and a health certificate called *certificat phyto sanitaire*. Any nonconforming bags of cloves were rejected at dockside, under testing and shipping procedures established by the International Chamber of Commerce in Paris.

Like all commodities, the cloves were sold against documents called bills of lading. When the documents are physically transferred, ownership or title to the goods passes. N-Ren also insisted that local weights govern sales to the trading company in Europe because cloves are hydroscopic (they take on weight and water in a tropical climate by up to 3 percent and lose weight in a drier climate).

Snyder found several buyers, the most prominent being Catz International, a spice trading company in Rotterdam. Catz also had a representative at dockside who agreed to buy a part of the cargo for a set price. World prices at the time were slightly under $10.00 per kilo. N-Ren thus took title to the whole shipment with only part of it presold. Being a skillful trading company, Catz knew the price would probably keep falling. They wanted N-Ren to hold a portion of the cargo, not presold, at dockside in Rotterdam for their account and risk, selling to Catz from the bonded warehouse. Catz knew it could buy this dockside portion at steadily lower prices and only as they found their own subsequent buyers. In any event, at least the cargo stored in the warehouse was duty-free. Taxes were not paid until the cloves were sold by Catz to wholesale buyers, long after N-Ren was out of the transaction.

SHIPMENTS

To guarantee payment to N-Ren, Catz opened up a letter of credit (L/C) with its bank, Credit Anstalt, in London; the L/C was confirmed by the American Express bank in Hamburg. Once the ship arrived at Rotterdam, documents were presented to Credit Anstalt in London, and it immediately paid N-Ren under the L/C.

The total value of this first shipment was in the area of $10 million. The Italian captain docked his ship and, under pressure to meet another shipping schedule, proceeded to unload his cargo in the rain even though it is well known that water damages cloves. He claimed that his contract called for him to unload, not to wait for a change in weather. Brown was at dockside for a full week and repeatedly argued with the captain to stop unloading, but to no avail. Some of the cloves were damaged, and a few of the 50-kilo jute bags were dissolved when the contents spilled out. The bonded warehouse, De Visser, which had worked with Catz before, helped get the insurance process and evaluation started and called in a specialized kiln company to dry and rebag the cloves where necessary. The insurance people investigated and segregated the damaged portion. A good salvage job was done, and it was later possible to sell the damaged portion at a discount. An exhaustive arbitration process concluded with an assessment by an "alleged" Parisian expert who placed a lower value on the damage than N-Ren wanted. About a year later, Hart agreed by phone with the adjuster on a claim payment approximating the difference in the cloves' full market value and the price brought by the spoiled portion. The claim was in the range of several hundred thousand dollars.

The next shipment of cloves, about 2,000 tons and also valued at approximately $10 million, was completed in April 1984. Everything went more or less smoothly.

A third shipment of similar value in late 1985 had two new difficulties. First, N-Ren's good experiences with the buyers led them to work directly with the trading companies for payment on a portion of the cloves shipment. The savings of not having to bear the cost of letters of credit were passed on to N-Ren. However, Hart recommended against this unless the relationship was quite strong and the trading knowledge high.

The second difficulty occurred when the shipping vessel failed to appear in Rotterdam at the appointed time. Hart tracked the vessel down only to discover it had docked at a small port north of Lisbon. Use of the vessel's time had come under legal dispute, involving the complexity of overlapping leases. Don went to Hamburg to meet with the owners and lawyers. To get the vessel released he had to arrange for the payment of tribute to the owners from all of the trading companies with cargo on board. (The French, Swiss, and West German companies had ground nuts, aluminum ingots, and steel, respectively.) N-Ren was upset with the shipping agent out of Hamburg for alleging that use of the ship was free and clear. N-Ren believes that if it had worked directly with the shipping company, such a problem would have been foreseen before contracts for the vessel's use were signed.

A fourth shipment of cloves took place in early 1988. Even though the price of cloves had continued to fall, a number of buyers including Catz were interested. (One of the largest buyers of cloves, Indonesia, which puts the spice in cigarettes, began to produce locally, driving the price down further.) Snyder was optimistic that finishing touches could be put on the plant. Both N-Ren and its joint venture partner, the government, hoped surplus funds from this sale would give the plant operating capital during its early years of production.

LESSONS TO BE LEARNED

There are lessons from this barter transaction that emphasize creativity and attention to meticulous detail. Snyder's persistence in meeting with senior officials of Madagascar, including ministers, was certainly one driving force in this transaction. Another was the falling price situation for cloves, where a glut of the commodity created a fertile environment for trading assistance to be offered. The barter solved not only the repayment problem, but a difficult marketing problem for a commodity in oversupply. Madagascar found a way to generate the foreign exchange to pay for the completion of a critical project. It did this without having to remit that exchange through the central bank, where other lenders, commercial banks, the International Monetary Fund, and the World Bank, might also want to claim it. The dilemma of which old debts to pay is never easily solved for many Third World countries.

Several lessons are also learned about the technique of structuring a barter sale. The company seeking to barter should arrange to sell the commodity on the same terms as when purchasing or on less stringent terms. For example, the weight that governs price should be the shipping weight at the port of departure rather than the cargo's weight at the port of arrival, which is probably less. Hart stressed that "the whole deal is in the base countertrade contract and in the letter of credit." Careful attention must be paid to the language and documentation for both. Shipping insurance covered the damage to the cloves caused by the rain, but not delays caused when lease disputes made the ship's captain dock in Portugal. Direct negotiations for a vessel without an agent may have solved that problem.

Preselling at least a portion of the cloves helped reduce N-Ren's risk in accepting title. This part could be sold by N-Ren to Catz on what is called *a back-to-back basis*. N-Ren bought cloves from the seller knowing it had a certain quantity presold to Catz and other buyers. Having buyers' representatives and N-Ren there at Tamatave to agree on quality and to supervise documentation for loading was essential. Snyder, Hart, Brown, and their colleagues monitored the transactions at every step of the way, solving problems and keeping the transactions under control.

Chapter Nine

Emphasis of Policy in Latin America

*"I wish I could tell you about our barter of
a power generator for coffee to a South American
country. The deal was fabulous."*
—Director of Countertrade for Westinghouse

OFFICIAL POLICY

With the major exception of Brazil, virtually every country in Latin America has an official policy calling for countertrade on major transactions. We have seen that even Brazil has allowed selected oil transactions. These countertrade policies dictate that a company wishing to import into a Latin American country must generate exports from that country. For example, the Ministry of Economic Development in Colombia published a decree (number 370) of February 15, 1984: "By which barter, compensation and triangular trade operations are established and regulated." An import board called INCOMEX was set up to make sure that importers guarantee that a corresponding export takes place, reimbursing INCOMEX if it does not. Under this policy Colombia bought cars from Renault for coffee in a transaction much criticized in the French press. Colombia has also traded coffee and bananas to the Soviet Union for manufactured goods.

The chief financial officer (CFO) of a major U.S. company illustrated colorfully the Latin American countertrade policy with an example in Mexico. The manager of a paper plant got into trouble by using corporate funds to buy hot peppers for export without authorization from the parent company. The CFO wanted to know why in the world he was buying hot peppers. The plant manager explained that the only way to import into Mexico the necessary chemicals for papermaking was to develop some kind of export. He felt he had to take matters into his own hands. The CFO chewed him out and then said: "Fine. Just tell me next time before you buy the hot peppers."

Many of the transactions in Latin America are of this sort, where an import must be linked according to government policy to a specially generated export.

In 1978, Ecuador became one of the first South American countries to develop a countertrade policy. Several of Ecuador's strong export products were made ineligible for countertrade—namely oil and oil byproducts, coffee, cocoa, shrimp, frozen fish, and bananas. Latin American countries often exclude their more valuable major commodities from countertrade transactions, preferring to sell them directly for cash. Sugar was not on Ecuador's prohibited list and in 1986 was involved in a curious transaction worth $8 million. Ecuador imported cheap sugar but exported its own higher quality product to the United States at a higher price in order not to lose its performance record for the purpose of calculating U.S. import quotas in future years (see Ref. 5, p. 9). Not every trade going into Ecuador is to support countertrade. One official estimated that perhaps only 5 percent (representing $25–30 million per year) of all trade was on a countertrade basis.

The myriad countertrade transactions in Latin America are too numerous to list here. The following examples should give an idea of the extent of countertrade practiced. The Argentine grain board traded grain for fertilizer. Peru countertraded textiles, canned tuna, juices, and furniture to the Soviet Union to reduce debt. Chile, seeking to avoid countertrading its valuable mineral resources such as copper, has exchanged fruit and vegetables for light manufactured products with Argentina and Brazil.

Such transactions have a common structure. They are permitted and regulated by official policy. Approval must be granted by both an import board for traded products to enter the country and by the central bank to allow valuable hard currency to leave the country.

BLOCKED CURRENCY

In addition to the above type of barter transaction where the goal is to export to the Latin American country, U.S. corporations have occasionally used countertrade to get "blocked currency" out of the country. Most Latin American countries have "blocked" their local currency in the sense of forbidding its conversion into dollars or some other hard currencies that can be taken freely out of the country. In the last decade, U.S. companies and banks have lost tens of millions of dollars in this fashion. On rare occasions, they have been successful in getting permission to buy export products for local currency and then receiving dollars when these products are sold on the world market. One large U.S. corporation was able to get its blocked currency out of Mexico in this manner through the purchase of consumer products. In Colombia, a U.S. company used its blocked currency to pay local expenses including air travel to and from the country.

The problem of blocked currency has been especially severe for Brazil. To alleviate one part of the problem, Brazil created ORTNs, which are cruzeriro savings bonds that float upward almost on a par with an inflation running typically over 200 percent. However, such bonds are only a partial solution because they must be kept in Brazilian banks. Companies and individuals look almost desperately for ways to convert local currency into dollars and to get these dollars out of the country. Some of their schemes are legendary. One approach is for the company to invest its cruzeriros locally, in hotel or factory projects, in order to take a dollar tax credit back in the United States. Another approach is to swap local currency loans between two entities in Brazil for dollar loans from their parent in the United States. It is, of course, possible to buy dollars on the "parallel" or black market and carry them out of the country, but the central bank would put a stop to systematic violations. One unusual scheme that allegedly worked came about when several clever entrepreneurs found a loophole in Brazilian law that allowed race horses to be imported. The entrepreneurs paid huge prices for breeding stock in Lexington, Kentucky, and then arranged for the overpayment to go into a U.S. bank. The animals mysteriously died in Brazil before their real value could be discovered. The central bank quickly closed this import loophole.

A great many U.S. and foreign companies have expressed keen interest in using countertrade to take their blocked currency out of Brazil. The blocked currency problem would probably be alleviated even if Brazil limited exports to priority manufactured goods, excluding its more valuable commodities. For the time being, however, Cacex (the Brazilian export agency based in Rio) will not grant export licenses for any products purchased with local currency.

The Brazilian central bank maintains that International Monetary Fund (IMF) guidelines prohibit countertrade by requiring the central bank to collect all foreign exchange proceeds for repayment of Brazil's massive debt. Businesspeople and commercial bankers both in and out of Brazil argue that using local currency to purchase exports would create jobs and not diminish Brazil's existing export flow. They very much wish the IMF would reverse its policy against countertrade, allowing countries undergoing an IMF restructuring to permit the use of blocked currency for the purchase of export products.

OFFSET COMMITMENT

Within Latin America, another type of countertrade, similar to offset in the European military sense, has begun to develop in certain instances for major purchases. Unlike barter transactions where the export and import are closely linked in time, the offset commitment takes place over a period of several years on a larger scale.

Francis Hamilton of the World Bank (formerly with the British investment banking firm of Samuel Montague) explained the concept of such a transaction in Uruguay. In 1984, several U.S. and European companies competed for a lucrative $90 million telephone switching system in Uruguay. The eventual winner, Ericsson of Sweden and its Brazilian subsidiary, triumphed mainly for two reasons.

First, Ericsson made the best offer of countertrade and the most convincing offer it could to implement the countertrade proposal. Hamilton put together the countertrade effort for Montague. On behalf of Ericsson, the investment bank offered Uruguay 100 percent offset, which of course meant a commitment to export the full sales contract value of $90 million worth of Uruguayan products such as beef, leather products, and fish. Hamilton convincingly proposed to do this through Surinvest, a joint venture trading and financing house established in Montevideo by Samuel Montague and Uruguayan partners. Surinvest has continued to fulfill the offset commitment successfully, and Montague considers the transaction one of the most profitable Surinvest has ever undertaken.

A second reason for Ericsson's success was its very attractive financing, export credit, provided at subsidized rates from the Swedish and Brazilian governments. The United States government would normally offer such credit through the U.S. Export-Import Bank (Eximbank). However, Eximbank as discussed in Chapter 2 had its loan capability sharply cut back during the early Reagan Administration and was not able to offer competitive financing. This Administration, led by the Treasury Department, practiced a policy of discouraging countertrade transactions and making it difficult for Eximbank to lend in situations where countertrade was involved. As one vice president of Eximbank explained: "If countertrade is brought into an Eximbank financing, the Treasury Department would get heartburn. We now have to disclose everything to the Treasury about the countertrade portion of a transaction. Treasury objections to countertrade will probably kill the deal."

A basic point here is that a more supportive financing position by the United States government, tolerating and encouraging countertrade where necessary, might have won this transaction for the U.S. competitor. The Europeans in this sale presented a more aggressive and clever mix of government-supported financing and countertrade.

COUNTERTRADE NEEDS HELP

Countertrade by itself cannot win a transaction, especially if the bank financing supporting this transaction is uncompetitive. Homing in on this issue, many banks have moved aggressively to develop creative financing expertise in support of countertrade transactions as an attractive business. For example, the investment bank, First Boston, once created a joint venture with a New York countertrade company, MG Services, to explore this type of creative financing (often called financial engineering). A few large banks are trying to mix countertrade and financing through their small trading companies established under the Export Trading Company Act.

Especially in South America, the money center banks on their own are pursuing a recently popular form of countertrade called a debt-equity swap to alleviate country debt burden problems. Several money center banks (i.e., very large banks such as Citibank, Chase) in the United States have chosen to write down billions in nonperforming loans to this region. In a few cases, the Latin American country has been able to sell these loans to investors, who then convert them into either domestic, local currency loans, or direct equity investment in that country. On some occasions, the investors have been U.S. money center banks themselves. Chile has begun such a program and has reported successfully slicing off $450 million from its foreign debt of about $20 billion. The rich natural resources and mining industries of Chile make it attractive for this sort of scheme, which is basically an investment in the country's future.

Early in 1988, Argentina began its debt-equity swap program, designed to give lenders the option of converting bad debts into local currency at a discount. Under this program local currency must be invested in projects in Argentina. If the projects generate foreign exchange, the investor may be eligible to transfer a portion of his earnings out of the country through foreign investment regulations. The investor also buys an equity position through a debt-equity swap, giving some protection against soaring Argentine inflation. When the Argentine peso later becomes fully convertible, then this equity position can be sold and transferred out of the country if the investor chooses. The Argentine debt-equity program is seeking to transform $1.9 billion of foreign debt in this way over a five-year period. So far, investors have proposed over $200 million for conversion and investment in local projects, surpassing the expectation of Argentine officials.

Conservation International, a Washington-based conservation group, structured an unusual debt swap in Bolivia by agreeing to purchase and forgive $650,000 of the country's debt in return for the establishment of three conservation areas of four million acres in the Amazonian rain forest.[6]

One of the appeals of countertrade is that its flexibility gives the skilled dealmaker more options to structure something of real interest and benefit especially to countries that consider themselves in difficulty. In Jamaica, the United States government bartered a portion of its surplus milk and food stores for aluminum, demonstrating the feasibility of this technique on a government basis for other countries elsewhere in the world in similar economic difficulty.

To encourage U.S. investment in the face of mounting economic problems, Mexico has recently developed an In-Bond program that could set an important precedent for other countries. The program draws on several creative approaches, including provisions in the U.S. Tariff Code exempting Mexican exports except for value added, the concept of a debt-equity swap, and finally the concept of a duty-free zone. Under this program, as explained by Robert M. Shipley, the U.S. commercial officer in Mexico City, a U.S. company, ACS of Rhode Island, was able to spend slightly over $1 million for a greater value of land and a building in a designated area. ACS also received $2 million in Mexican pesos to spend locally. They will import copper wire into the new Mexican facility and will export the cord used in stereo headphones. This program proved attractive to the company because they will pay a tariff only on the value added to the copper wire imported, and because of the low labor costs in Mexico. Under the new program, Mexico also permits 100 percent ownership of a local company if it is in a duty-free area and other criteria are met. The concepts developed in Mexico would be interesting if applied in other Latin American countries like Brazil where foreign investment, not to mention lending, has been cut back.

SUMMARY

In Latin America we are dealing in general with more formalized government requirements calling for a balancing of exports and imports, in counterpurchase fashion. A few military-style offsets are also coming into effect, lasting for several years, in connection with sizable purchases as happened in Uruguay. As in Africa, the use of commodities and minerals is prevalent. Even the most exportable commodities (e.g., grain in Argentina or coffee in Colombia) have been used in countertrade, despite sensitivities that they should be excluded.

Debt-equity swaps are fundamentally a countertrade concept and have come into play in at least two key South American countries with serious debt problems, Argentina and Chile. I am surprised that countertrade has not been used more extensively to resolve some of the blocked currency problems, especially in Brazil. There is little risk in allowing foreign corporations with frozen accounts to buy Brazilian products for export, if this process is managed and properly spread out over time. Foreign exchange generated from the sales could be kept by the corporations whose assets were blocked. Unfreezing these accounts to permit countertrade might actually encourage new foreign investment in Brazil over time, especially if the surge in exports, resulting from the spending of frozen funds, led to more currency stabilization and ultimately full convertibility. I hope the IMF will thus reverse its policy against countertrade as a tool relieving blocked currency situations, especially in Latin America. A freer policy on countertrade would be beneficial both to investing companies and to the countries themselves.

Chapter Ten

Asia: The New Force in Countertrade

"Negative neutrality."
—Response of Japanese official at the Ministry of Trade
and Industry (MITI) when asked his
country's position on countertrade

COUNTERTRADE COMES TO JAPAN

During the years 1975 to 1980, when European countries were signing their first major offset transactions, the Japanese were apparently reluctant to adopt countertrade practices, preferring straight cash for product sales. As a prospering country, riding an export and manufacturing boom, Japan had little need for countertrade. Its generous, low-interest financing enabled it to be repaid in currency rather than product. This situation is now beginning to change. Because huge Japanese trading companies with their large world networks and billions of dollars in turnover are so naturally positioned, they can see the potential benefits from the countertrading surge sweeping through the world. Mitsubishi supposedly did over a billion dollars' worth of countertrade business in 1987 alone.

Even the military offset situation is changing. Since the early 1980s, when Japan requested no military offsets, Japanese policymakers have emphasized the technology transfer aspect of offsets and have been very forceful and successful in this area especially since 1985.

The 1985 OMB report lists no military offset transactions for Japan during the period of 1980–1984, and relatively small amounts for other Asian countries (see Table 3).[2] Aside from $1.2 billion in Australia, there were $1.2 million in New Zealand, $45 million in Singapore, $0.1 million in the Philippines, and $156 million in South Korea. The pace of countertrading has increased markedly since 1985 for other Asian countries as it has for Japan.

The Japanese have begun to use barter and counter-purchase to supplement their aggressive, low-interest, export financing and government-to-government grants. On several occasions, for example, Japanese companies have accepted rice from Malaysia for manufactured goods, even though such countertrade is technically disparaged by their government. U.S. manufacturing companies have often brought in Japanese trading companies like C. Itoh, Mitsubishi, Sumitomo, and Mitsui to support the countertrading requirements of larger transactions because of their expertise. I have mentioned that C. Itoh traded oil for Boeing's 747 barter sale to Saudi Arabia (Chapter 6). Chuck Martin, the director of International Licensing and Countertrade at Westinghouse, said his firm had used Japanese trading companies several times to move commodities accepted in barter transactions: "In these situations we always give the Japanese a chance to bid. Their prices are often very competitive, and their networks are incredible."

In the People's Republic of China especially, where the Japanese have geographic and linguistic ties, one experienced trader observed: "The Japanese trading companies are so well-positioned that foreign firms may have a hard time cutting into their market." Many of Japan's mining and processing investments in China are on a countertrade basis, where the Chinese outlay of cash is zero or minimal, and the investor is repaid by taking back mineral ore or processed goods. Actually, as an official of the mining company Amax described to me, there is a tradition in the mining industry for services to be repaid with a portion of the product. In China, the Japanese have mastered this technique, called compensation.

MILITARY OFFSETS

In the area of military offsets, the Japanese are catching on from Europe and have developed a policy. Eileen White reported that since 1982 the Japanese have licensed technology from U.S. companies for 12 different weapons, including missiles. Some of these agreements were not included in the 1985 OMB study. Since they involved technology transfer and not trading, they may have mistakenly not been included in the list of offset transactions. Japan's military research has emphasized missiles that would be potential competitors to the U.S.-made Stinger, Sidewinder, and Harpoon in the lucrative international market.[3] In one of these weapons transactions, Japan recently bought F-15 military aircraft from McDonnell-Douglas. They requested and received a technology transfer package that according to one newspaper account would help further the Japanese objective of developing an industry capable of capturing 30 percent of the defense aerospace market in the next decade.[7] The issue of Japan's use of offsets to secure technology transfer came up repeatedly in testimony to the U.S. Senate Armed Services Committee in March 1988. The debate focused on General Dynamics' sale of a version of the F-16 called the FSX to the Japanese government through an arrangement allowing Mitsubishi great access to F-16 technology.

The origins for aerospace co-production agreements with Japan have a sensible foundation in a package, negotiated with Boeing in the late 1970s, concerning the Boeing 767 commercial aircraft.

Japan was able to use its leverage as a large potential market for both the 767 and the competing Airbus to get a co-production agreement from Boeing calling for a modest 6 percent participation in the manufacture of certain components for the aircraft. (Boeing also offered 5 percent to the Italians.) From the Japanese point of view, it was a significant step in building an aerospace industry. But from Boeing's position it was a stroke of genius to accommodate Japanese domestic needs by offering them a role in the manufacture of the plane. Japan and Boeing accomplished the objectives of offset informally without representing it as such. Crucially, Boeing also received a financing commitment from Japanese banks, including the Japan Export-Import Bank, to offer attractive financing in support of sales worldwide. Allowing some Japanese participation in the 767 was thus a way of thinking countertrade. Boeing gained not only valuable market share, but access to financing in the major capital markets of Tokyo, financing that is still important to the 767 program.

COUNTERTRADE IN THE PEOPLE'S REPUBLIC OF CHINA

The Chinese are getting into the offset picture too, with the Peace Pearl program, the first United States government-sponsored defense transaction with the People's Republic of China. Rockwell, Boeing, and Grumman are competing for the $500 million sale, which is to be supported by United States government Foreign Ministry Sales (FMS) credits. The program is to supply 50 kits to modify the avionics and fire control of some aging Chinese jets. Despite insistence by the U.S. Department of Defense on no countertrade (under the Duncan ruling by the Department prohibiting it in FMS-supported sales), the Chinese are requiring 30 percent offset of a six- to seven-year term, and the U.S. companies are preparing their offers.

In China, the more typical countertrade transaction is the kind of compensation agreement mentioned earlier for the Japanese. U.S. companies have also signed such agreements. In a much publicized transaction, Occidental Petroleum got a long-term contract to take back ore and refined minerals in return for developing a large mining facility.

Barter and counterpurchase arrangements are also carried out with Chinese companies. A senior officer at Hercules mentioned that his company had been buying gum resin directly from China for years. Another officer, the company's treasurer, found out one day he could buy the gum resin more cheaply not in China, the supplier, but in Hong Kong. He could not understand why until the senior officer explained the situation. Traders in Hong Kong were buying gum resin below market prices in order to fulfill other barter and counterpurchase arrangements. They would sell gum resin coming out of China at a steep discount, building up large volumes, in order to use those credits for exporting other products back into China. In short, it was cheaper to buy gum resin from the Hong Kong countertrader than the source in China.

In another case of barter, Green Island Cement, a Hutchison Group sister company, is to provide 50,000 tons of cement to the China National Mineral and Metals Import Export Corporation (MIN/NET). On the other side of the barter sale, China National Coal Import Export Corporation (CNCIEC) is to sell 50,000 tons of coal for distribution through Total Energy Resources (Hong Kong) Ltd., a joint venture between Hutchison and Total (the French petroleum company). Simon To, the managing director of Hutchison, said it took nearly a year to complete this very complicated transaction. He feels the effort was justifiable because of the precedent established, giving him the option of trading another 150,000 tons of coal and cement. There were a number of problems to be solved. First, he convinced the state planning commission of the central government that the sale made sense even though CNCIEC was unhappy about losing valuable foreign exchange to another Chinese company. A separate central office, the State Supplies Bureau, took charge of distributing the cement. Second, China normally exports coal to countries that are prepared to pay 10 percent over market price. Because CNCIEC refused to lower its price, Hutchison had to compensate by raising the price of the cement. Third, MIN/NET insisted it needed the cement two months before CNCIEC was prepared to deliver the coal. Finally, the port authorities would not unload the coal since they could not qualify for unloading bonuses associated with foreign cargoes (see Ref. 5, p. 10).

From this and other examples, it appears that while companies may want to countertrade with China, the Chinese have not yet structured a system to handle it well. Several executives describe coordination problems among agencies and report that the Chinese do not always make clear whether a company is dealing with the state or with a municipality.

COUNTERTRADE IN OTHER ASIAN COUNTRIES

Indonesia

The first country to develop a countertrade policy in Asia was neither China nor Japan, but Indonesia in the late 1970s. The Indonesian system requires a counterpurchase commitment of 100 percent for any significant import (over about $750,000). Indonesia has been criticized for awarding credit to all exports, including its highly prized rubber, coffee, and plywood. Such a system of linking existing exports to imports, without adding incremental value, has been called "trading with mirrors." In Indonesia, there are substantial penalties of up to 50 percent of contract value for the importer who does not buy an equal value of export items, or at least link them in this "mirror" sense. By 1983, Indonesia had generated $200 million in countertrade, and the pace has since accelerated. In one large transaction, International Commodities Export Corporation (ICEC), a subsidiary of Donaldson Lufkin and Jenrette, sold some $45 million of fertilizer to Indonesia and bought the same value of rubber, cocoa, coffee, and other commodities.[8] Emil Finley, the president of ICEC, emphasized proudly the triangular nature of the trade. Two years earlier, he had taken urea from Rumania in a countertrade, and was able to ship some of the urea to Indonesia as part of the fertilizer contract.

Malaysia

In 1983/1984, Malaysia introduced a countertrade policy similar to Indonesia's and has suggested it will try to link government purchases with exports from a list of products it wishes to promote. The list comprised 28 pages and, fortunately for foreign importers, seemed to include virtually every Malaysian export except for its most valuable commodity, unprocessed rubber. Malaysia stresses a countertrade system in the sense of linked purchases or counterpurchases of exports and imports. Both Indonesia and Malaysia have bartered with Eastern Europe in the direct sense of swapping equal values of rubber, for example, to obtain fertilizer, petrochemicals, and machinery.

Philippines

The Philippines has a more severe debt crisis than either Malaysia or Indonesia and has taken counterpurchase more seriously, making sure that importers generate incremental exports that would not otherwise take place and where the hard currency thus generated is used to pay for the import. In another policy reminiscent of many Latin American economies, the Philippines negotiated debt-equity swap arrangements with the IFC/World Bank and a consortium of commercial banks and investment banks.

India

There appear to have been no significant military offset agreements in the Philippines, nor in the subcontinent countries of India, Pakistan, Bangladesh, and Sri Lanka. There have, however, been some spectacular countertrades between these subcontinent countries and their trading partners. India and the Soviet Union trade with each other in the context of bilateral agreements where the trading flows are monitored and kept balanced on a yearly basis in clearing account units (see Chapter 12). Helene Curtis sold 60,000 tons of shampoo to the Soviets under one of these rupee–ruble clearing account agreements. To do this, the firm sourced (produced) the shampoo in its 49 percent owned Indian subsidiary factory. The "Indian" origin of the product made it eligible for export under the bilateral agreement with the Soviet Union. Helene Curtis earned the foreign exchange from India by virtue of its 49 percent stake in the subsidiary. India has also countertraded textiles and manufactured products to North Korea for cement and to Vietnam, Cambodia, and Laos for rice.

Pakistan

Pakistan confines its barter agreements to Eastern Europe and the Soviet Union. An embassy official described the trading conceptually: "Pakistan trades textiles, leather goods, sporting goods, machine tools, and surgical instruments for machinery, fertilizer, and chemicals." Bilateral protocols are signed each year, and there are annual accounting sessions to balance the trade flows.

Bangladesh and Sri Lanka

Bangladesh, similarly, confines its barter to yearly bilateral agreements with the Soviets and Eastern Europe, trading products such as rope and cord for food and light machinery. Sri Lanka has bartered small amounts of rice or rubber to the Eastern Bloc as well.

Taiwan and South Korea

Taiwan has been reluctant to countertrade, preferring to operate on a cash basis. However, in the area of military sales it has been the beneficiary of co-production in Taiwan and technology transfer from U.S. corporations. South Korea has emphasized the military offset area of countertrade.

North Korea

There is on the record a fascinating barter arrangement with North Korea, involving parties in the United States, France, and Switzerland, with the Swiss shipping wheat to Korea and the latter shipping rice. The difficulties encountered in the Chinese cement-for-coal deal (page 120) pale by comparison with this transaction, which I have included to show the ultimate potential of countertrade as a problem-solver.[9]

The transaction proceeded like this. Both the North Korean trade agency and the Swiss trading firm worked through a French broker, which used a U.S. trading company as a facilitator. The North Koreans traded rice and received wheat. The Swiss traded wheat from various origins to receive the North Korean rice for resale to various destinations. Regardless of world spot prices for wheat or rice, the exchange ratio was fixed at 1.5 parts wheat out of the North Korean port of Nampo, exchanged for one part rice at Nampo. Under the agreement, 90,000 tons of wheat were shipped in and 60,000 tons of rice were shipped out. The wheat had to be equal to U.S. number four or better quality soft wheat with the rice equal to U.S. number three quality, milled and packaged in 50 net kilogram bags. Both parties had to provide a standby guarantee (through a French bank of the broker's choice) equal to one-fourth the value of the goods received and to be drawn against if the other contractor failed to meet the shipment deadlines. For this purpose, the rice was valued at 1,800 French francs and the wheat at 1,200 French francs. The weight and final quality at shipment were to be verified with certificates issued by Surveillance Général of Geneva. The problems in this transaction were almost overwhelming. It was hard to find vessels going to North Korea, let alone vessels that could meet shipping deadlines. News that any of the parties were trading with North Korea would damage trade relations in the far more lucrative South Korean market. Air transportation for surveyors and contractors in and out of North Korea was also quite infrequent. For security reasons, North Korea made no public data available about constantly changing port and weather conditions. Inspectors were not permitted to check goods on shore, and indeed no crew member was permitted ashore. The North Koreans claimed not to be familiar with international standards for commodities. There were, in brief, "endless headaches in execution, communication, and transportation." However, there were high margins for the Western parties, a new market was opened, and an opportunity was provided to market lower quality European wheat that might have been used elsewhere as animal food at a much lower value.

COUNTERTRADE ACCELERATES

Generally, the pace of countertrade in Asia is accelerating, with the countries themselves looking increasingly for packages of technology transfer, co-production, and subcontracting. Japan is, of course, the largest trading market and its companies are increasingly drawn into countertrade. Yet the People's Republic of China has become the largest market where countertrading itself is common, if not required, to do business. For example, the largest technology transfer sale to China was recently announced by Gareth Chang, president of McDonnell-Douglas China, in support of a 25-plane fleet of commercial aircraft called the twin-jet MD-82.[10] The first U.S. jetliner, built in China by Chinese workers, rolled off the assembly line on July 31, 1987. The translation problems alone were formidable, with 80 interpreters working with U.S. engineers and 300 persons doing technical translations. The co-production program in Shanghai created 2,000 jobs for Chinese workers and another 1,000 will be added. The technology transfer package has allowed 30 Chinese engineers to study and work on jet propulsion at Douglas Aircraft in Long Beach, California (the commercial aircraft division of McDonnell-Douglas). Boeing had previously sold more than 50 commercial aircraft to China; McDonnell-Douglas had sold five. Both companies believe the aircraft market in China will be enormous and are competing for a new order of 150 planes worth about $4 billion to be built in Chinese co-production factories in the 1990s.

SUMMARY

It is not easy to summarize countertrade patterns in Asia because of the great variety and rapid development of

countertrade policies and techniques. Countertrade is practiced in all Asian countries with the possible exception of
Taiwan, and even the Taiwanese have benefited from co-production agreements. After this observation, generalization
becomes difficult.

At one extreme, the Japanese have become a countertrade force in two major ways. First, as a growing and major
purchaser of defense systems from the West, they have been
able to extract technology transfer and co-production agreements with increasing zeal and success. This process is
facilitated by the veiled threat, probably credible, that unless
the winning bidders go along with these schemes, the
Japanese will accelerate their own military production capacity and compete for exports. Second, the Japanese trading
companies, building their networks for over a century in
some cases, are well positioned to provide countertrade
services for themselves and clients around the world.

At the other extreme, the Philippines, struggling to re-
stabilize after the ouster of Ferdinand Marcos, needs counterpurchase to build foreign exchange reserves and regain its
momentum in economic development.

The huge Chinese market has found various forms of
countertrade essential, especially in the absence of a convertible currency. Ironically, like Japan, the developed
economies of South Korea, Singapore, and Hong Kong have
found that commercial countertrade (to increase market
share) and military offsets (to gain technology transfer and
co-production) are a very successful way of doing business.

The experiences of other Asian countries, from India to
Indonesia, have produced enough positive results to promote
the technique, and the proliferation of countertrade shows
every sign of continuing.

Chapter Eleven

When Everything
Is Negotiable:
The Case of Yugoslavia

*"We were so successful with our first joint venture
that we are looking to set up others in Yugoslavia."*
—DON OGLESBY, Chairman, Peak Technologies Inc., Scottsdale, Arizona

INTRODUCTION

Yugoslavia is famous to students of countertrade because of a sale in which McDonnell-Douglas agreed to accept a large quantity of ham as well as other items to generate foreign exchange for the purpose of purchasing commercial aircraft. The ham transaction, discussed in Chapter 14, illustrates the one principle of the informal counterpurchase system in Yugoslavia that is often frustrating to U.S. companies. There are basically no uniformly applied rules, and everything is subject to negotiation.

The strong sense of regionalism in Yugoslavia is another complicating factor. Yugoslavia's federal government sometimes likes to delegate responsibilities to local authorities in the six republics and two autonomous provinces. There are no precise procedures to be followed, and therefore company officials often do not know whether to talk to the officials at the regional level or at the federal level in Belgrade. Yet, most companies very quickly discover that counterpurchase on some basis is a necessity. Unless the U.S. company can generate a sale of some Yugoslav export, there is no foreign exchange available to pay for the product a U.S. company wants to sell into the country.

ABSENCE OF RULES

What is a U.S. company to do? In one sense, the absence of rules creates a positive climate for entrepreneurs to negotiate favorable business arrangements.

For example, Don Oglesby, the chairman of Peak Technology Ventures, Inc. in Scottsdale, Arizona, found the informal counterpurchase requirements in Yugoslavia to be a major factor for his company's success there. Two years ago Oglesby established a joint venture with a Yugoslav company, Magmedia Technologies, in the town of Metkovic located in Yugoslavia's Republic of Croatia. The company manufactures floppy disks for computers using U.S. manufacturing and testing equipment. The disks, in 8 in., $5\frac{1}{4}$ in., and $3\frac{1}{2}$ in. standard sizes, have been approved by the American National Standards Institute and its European counterpart.

The disks have also been approved by several companies in the United States who would view their purchases of them as a way to generate foreign exchange enabling the sale of other products into Yugoslavia. One major U.S. defense contractor has already begun buying the disks to satisfy its counterpurchase requirements.

JOINT VENTURE

Magmedia is also the only U.S.-sponsored joint venture to be located in a free trade zone, where components can be imported duty-free if they are assembled into exports. Like other Yugoslavian companies, the joint venture has to stand in line at a republic-level bank to get the foreign exchange necessary to buy imports. (The foreign exchange earned from its exports is potentially assigned to U.S. buyers of disks who have their own counterpurchase needs.)

The joint venture cleverly uses barter to avoid this problem of having to line up scarce foreign exchange to purchase the raw material imports necessary to make a disk. Peak Technologies, the joint venture partner, buys the raw material outside Yugoslavia using dollars. It ships the raw material to its joint venture partner, Magmedia, and accepts finished floppy disks in return as payment for the investment.

The company already employs 50 people and is sure to grow, Peak's chairman believes, because of the counterpurchase needs of major U.S. companies. To facilitate counterpurchase for U.S. customers, who buy directly from the factory, Magmedia makes the necessary contacts with the Yugoslav government. Oglesby says that whom to contact is the one trade secret about this transaction he will not reveal. For military customers, the contact is at the federal level; for commercial customers, the contacts will be at either the republic or the federal level. Encouraged by his success, Oglesby is trying to set up other joint ventures in Yugoslavia.

The experience of Peak Technologies illustrates a number of successful techniques for doing business in a country strapped for foreign exchange. The joint venture concept accommodates local needs for participation, providing an acceptable way to relate to Yugoslav authorities. It also provides a U.S. partner with access to foreign exchange. The need of many U.S. companies for counterpurchase provides a ready market for the disks that is potentially large. Peak's willingness to barter raw material into Yugoslavia for finished products is a way to put the factory into production. Peak and Magmedia have basically taken the obstacles to exporting into Yugoslavia and converted them into assets for a successful business.

Peak's American consultant, Jim Barkus of New York (retained to locate sales for disks among U.S. manufacturers needing counterpurchase in Yugoslavia), explains how he created a similar marketing triangle. Barkus advised a furniture importer to increase its purchases from Yugoslavia. He facilitated the arrangements with Yugoslav authorities he had known for years, and then introduced the importer to another U.S. company that wanted to export to the furniture maker in Yugoslavia. Such an increase could happen only if additional exports were generated from the furniture maker and the two transactions were linked together in the government's approval process. The U.S. purchaser was an importer of bookcases, so it was not hard to find suppliers of sandpaper, lacquer, glue, and veneer in the United States who wanted to export to the Yugoslav furniture maker.[11]

DIFFICULTIES

The difficulty of obtaining approval for a transaction from Yugoslav authorities should not be underestimated. A former colleague of mine talked about the struggles of a client of his, a defense company in the United Kingdom, to obtain counterpurchase exports in Yugoslavia as part of an offset arrangement. The offset called for some $3 million in exports and was reinforced with an onerous penalty in excess of 10 percent of the contract price. My colleague accepted the assignment of locating counterpurchase goods only after making two discoveries. First, as a military matter, the transaction required him to deal with federal authorities at a centralized level, rather than with one or more of the individual republics. Second, the Yugoslavs assured him that approval would be offered for any exports generated.

In fact, no matter what export my colleague proposed, the Yugoslavs turned him down. He finally concluded they may have been looking for a way to collect on the lucrative penalty in the contract, rather than for the exports generated through the offset. It goes without saying that companies seeking to negotiate an offset should keep penalties not only as low as possible, but low enough to prevent the penalty from being an attraction to the client in its own right.

A number of other difficulties have been reported by U.S. exporters. Sometimes the Yugoslavs want the offset or counterpurchase goods to come from the republic destined to receive the U.S. export. Yugoslav buyers (of U.S. goods and services) that do not export and are unable to generate foreign exchange directly have a tougher time getting foreign exchange than Yugoslav exporters. Under the Yugoslav foreign exchange law of 1986, exporting companies that need to import components for assembly into exports have the top priority for obtaining foreign exchange.

Even these top priority companies have to "stand in line" along with lower priority companies at the republic-level banks authorized to dispense foreign exchange. Getting foreign exchange credit at a bank, as it turns out, is not such an easy matter. The Yugoslav importer and the exporter in Yugoslavia generating the counterpurchase credit must agree in advance to associate their exports and imports, confirming the agreement with an exchange of paperwork that can be shown to government officials.

The 1986 law, which established priority levels for companies obtaining foreign exchange, also mandated that all companies earning foreign exchange remit it to an authorized republic bank within 60 days of receipt. Such a request is not unusual. Countries in Latin America with large foreign borrowing routinely do a similar thing, requiring that foreign exchange be handed over to the central bank. Unfortunately, Yugoslavia now also has soaring inflation, in the range of 170 percent. The exporter needing to buy back foreign exchange with dinars in order to pay for more imports of subcomponents must pay significantly more dinars to purchase the same amount of foreign exchange. One unintended consequence of the 1986 law was thus to fan the fires of inflation further by establishing incentives to avoid this costly exchange process. The law created incentives to produce for domestic consumption and disincentives to export.

Yugoslavia actively purchased U.S. exports in the 1970s, for example, a nuclear power plant from Westinghouse and commercial aircraft from McDonnell-Douglas. Economic difficulties have increased since a recession there in the early 1980s. The country continues to purchase from the United States and might gradually increase these imports once its difficulties are overcome.

SOVIET BLOC THROUGH YUGOSLAVIA

Another important reason to look at Yugoslavia is to introduce the subject of countertrade with Eastern Europe and the Soviet Union. Yugoslavia broke with the Soviet Union under President Tito and considers itself outside the Soviet Bloc. However, Yugoslavia carries out significant trade with Eastern Europe and the Soviet Union. The Yugoslav commercial attaché in Washington, D.C., proudly pointed out, for example, that his country has supplied the Soviet Union with numerous steam generators for nuclear power plants. By informally requiring counterpurchase for nearly all imports above $1 million, Yugoslavia's purchasing system resembles somewhat the more formally established counterpurchase system of its East European neighbors.

The Western company seeking to countertrade with Yugoslavia nevertheless faces a curious politico-economic situation different from the rest of Eastern Europe and the Soviet Union. The company deals less with the central federal government and more directly with the autonomous regional authorities and with the factories or the various trading companies that sometimes act as intermediaries. Ironically, this probably creates more rather than less bureaucracy because the federal government still can play a role. For example, before extending a loan to a Yugoslav borrower, the Export-Import Bank (Eximbank) during several years required a "super-guarantee" by the federal, central bank on top of the guarantee by the regional bank. This irritated the Yugoslavs who are proud of their decentralized approach, and they finally negotiated an end to the "super guarantee." Unfortunately, its demise came at the end of the 1970s, shortly before all Eximbank lending was cut back anyway.

Yugoslav companies are not "state-owned" but "worker-owned" and "worker-managed" as Yugoslavs are proud to point out, distinguishing them from those in the Soviet Union and much of Eastern Europe. The relative independence of Yugoslav companies makes them perhaps more entrepreneurial and easier to deal with directly, compared to companies elsewhere in Eastern Europe. Problems are more likely to arise in understanding the regional system, and decision-making in many companies is less centralized, paralleling the Yugoslav system of government where autonomous provinces and regions are emphasized within the central government.

Sales and purchases are sometimes facilitated by Yugoslav trading companies serving as agents on at least one side of a countertrade transaction. A former colleague of mine stated that while it is less expensive to purchase directly from a Yugoslav factory, it can be safer and more convenient in dealing with the bureaucracy to work through a trading company. Experience will dictate, he suggested, which path is better. These trading companies are somewhat like the centralized foreign trade organizations (FTOs) that are designated in Eastern Europe and the Soviet Union to carry out trading in selected sectors. Smaller trading companies specialize in areas such as textiles, metals, and food. Larger general trading companies, which are state-owned (such as Genex and Inex), have representative offices all over

Yugoslavia. Regardless of size, the trading companies assist in making contact with factories and in getting contracts approved by the authorities.

Yugoslav trade with the Soviet Union and East European countries is carried out in typical, more centralized East European fashion. Yugoslavia negotiates a general protocol, usually for five years, with its East Europe trading partners. Government representatives meet each year to negotiate new shopping lists that are gradually balanced in units called "clearing currency" or "clearing rubles." The accounting is clarified at these yearly bilateral meetings, and imbalances are corrected by adjustments in the shopping list for the upcoming year. According to one Yugoslav attaché, the Soviets "like to buy shoes, textiles, home appliances, and industrial goods." Yugoslavia receives items such as oil, raw materials, and certain manufactured items from the Soviet Union.

I am a little surprised at the amount of trade carried on between Yugoslavia and the Soviet Bloc, considering the break in political relations with the Soviet Union. In this context, an increase in trade with the United States would be desirable both economically and politically. More availability of export credit financing could help some, but this still does not solve the need under current Yugoslav policy to generate exports linked to imports. If the United States government had a trading company of its own, or at least an ownership position in one, trading could be directed toward Yugoslav products as a way of helping U.S. companies to sell into this and other nations where soaring inflation and blocked currency have made international commerce difficult.

Chapter Twelve

Countertrade as a Way of Life in Eastern Europe and the Soviet Union

*"When we barter rubber for manufactured
goods and consumer products, it is more
often with Eastern Europe rather than with Russia,
where the quality is not particularly good."*
—Malaysian Commercial Attaché in Washington, D.C.

ATTRACTION TO COUNTERTRADE

If the practice of countertrade is increasing in Asia, it is a way of life in the Eastern Bloc and the Soviet Union. Basically, this is because of a certain economic isolation of these countries, causing a lack of sufficient hard currency (i.e., dollars, pounds sterling, yen, etc.) in their central banks and the lack of easily convertible local currency. Most of the companies in this region are state-owned, and their trading is inherently centrally regulated. As it turns out, countertrading among these countries as a group is the easiest form of trading, and it is done on a government-to-government basis. There is, of course, a natural cultural and ideological attraction among the socialist countries to a system that fundamentally spurns capitalist currency.

Mostly since World War II, a unique system of bilateral clearing agreements has arisen among these countries and their closest trading partners. These agreements are fulfilled under a formal accounting system, renegotiated at regular intervals such as annually, where trading inflows and outflows are valued and recorded and must effectively balance out during the interval. Otherwise, one country will owe a debt to the other and must attempt to make it up during the next trading interval. The recorded values are called "clearing currency" and are often recorded as "clearing ruples," "clearing dollars," or some other appropriate currency. Whatever trade flows generate the clearing currency, whether importing or exporting, must be ultimately matched or balanced by trade that flows in the opposite direction.

The problem with this system is that it is self-perpetuating and on its own could never allow the Eastern Bloc countries to build up reserves of hard convertible currencies. Hard currency is never needed to settle the clearing account. Naturally, the Eastern Bloc countries try to export to the

West for valuable hard currency whenever possible, but much of their trading is still among themselves and is on the clearing currency basis.

One result of this system is to make trading at least conceptually easier with Third World countries than with the United States. Third World countries, even those with large private sectors such as India and Brazil, have more central control, state trading agencies, and a relative willingness to sign bilateral clearing agreements with Eastern Europe. In 1983, Brazil held a surplus of over $1 billion East European clearing dollars, and also piles of shoddy goods. Because of its rich natural resources, Brazil was able to export much more than it wanted to buy from Eastern Europe. Brazil's central bank governor, Carlos Langoni, said that even though he could extract a minimal benefit from the situation by including some of the clearing dollars in Brazil's official reserves, the country needed to avoid future imbalances in these bilateral clearing arrangements.[8]

COUNTERTRADE WITH EASTERN BLOC

Despite the existence of structures facilitating trade with the Third World, more Eastern Bloc trade is with Western Europe, probably because of geographic proximity and a more common orientation culturally. Pompiliu Verzariu, the U.S. Commerce Department's chief officer for monitoring countertrade, compiled numerous examples of countertrade transactions between the West and the Eastern Bloc from 1969 to 1978.[12] In Table 4, I have restructured Verzariu's information to show the trading patterns by country more clearly for this period of time. The list is not exhaustive and must be considered in this context.* Nevertheless, it is extensive and perhaps representative, and is at least indicative of the countertrade patterns among the countries in terms of relative numbers of transactions. It was not possible to weight the list by size of transactions because only some of the values were listed.

Out of the sample of 211 transactions, 156 were with Western Europe countries, 31 were with the United States, and 24 were with Japan. West Germany appeared to be most actively countertrading with the Eastern Bloc generally, with more than twice the examples of any other country. From this list, West Germany and Japan appeared to be more actively trading with the Soviet Union. Within the Eastern Bloc the United States appears to have countertraded most actively with Poland and Hungary, with whom cultural ties are closer possibly because of relatively larger immigrant populations in the United States.

Unlike much of the countertrade between the Eastern Bloc and the Third World, based on government-to-government clearing agreements, Western countertrade appears to be in some form of direct barter or counterpurchase between the Western corporation or trading company and the Eastern Bloc country. There appears to be little or no public evidence of clearing account arrangements between the Eastern Bloc and the United States, Japan, or Western Europe, and indeed there has been some opposition to such agreements. The Western corporate entity usually countertrades through a foreign trade organization (FTO) in the Eastern European country. There are often several FTOs in the country, oriented toward different industrial sectors. When

*In this sample three U.S./U.K. countertrade transactions were counted as U.S., one Denmark/France was counted as France, one France/Belgium as France, and one France/Austria/West Germany was counted as West Germany.

Table 4 COUNTERTRADE PATTERNS WITH EASTERN BLOC (1969–1978)

	BULGARIA	CZECHOSLOVAKIA	HUNGARY	POLAND	EAST GERMANY	RUMANIA	U.S.S.R.	TOTALS
United States	1		9	12	1		8	31
West Germany	2	1	16	9	6	2	17	53
France	1		4	9	3	1	7	25
Italy	1	1	3	2	2	1	9	19
Austria			6	3	3		4	16
Sweden		1	6					7
United Kingdom		1	3	4	1		2	11
Netherlands				2	1			3
Belgium			2		1		1	4
Norway			1					1
Finland			1		1		6	8
Japan		1	3	2		1	16	24
Denmark	1		1				1	4
Switzerland			3	1				5
TOTALS	7	5	53	52	19	4	71	211

countertrade originates in the Eastern European country, it is largely due to an import quota assigned to the FTO usually by the Ministry of Foreign Trade. Despite the similarity of overall structure in countertrading within Eastern Europe, there are subtle differences in each country, often reflecting something fundamental.

To capture the flavor of these differences, I spoke not only with traders in various corporations, but also with economic and commercial attachés at the embassies of Eastern European countries in Washington. For example, while these attachés admired Soviet space technology, they had an almost condescending attitude toward the Soviets' ability to produce consumer goods. In some respects they viewed the Soviet Union as a source of raw materials including oil, and often structured their countertrade agreements to purchase these basic materials with their own consumer goods and other manufactured items.

THE SOVIET UNION

United States trade with the Soviet Union has had its ups and downs. It is usually on a cash or partial cash basis rather than on a strictly countertrade basis. Soviet wheat purchases are for cash. Sales to the Soviet Union are monitored by the U.S. Department of Commerce, which must grant export licenses. Because of this, many sales in the computer and defense areas are strictly prohibited. Difficulties in U.S.– Soviet relations have brought about periodic embargoes, cutting off both grain shipments to the Soviet Union during the Carter Administration and U.S. participation in the natural gas pipeline to Western Europe.

Despite all the problems and barriers, opportunities for trade continue to exist. The Soviet center for trading with the

United States is the Amtorg Trading Company in New York. This is an umbrella organization of the representative offices for some 50 FTOs that specialize in various areas of Soviet exports. Most of these FTOs also have representative offices in Moscow.

In cases where dollars are not available, Soviet policy appears to encourage countertrade as a means of trade with the United States or Western Europe, and there are several notable examples. Probably the largest countertrade ever with the Soviet Union (worth up to $10 billion) is the natural gas pipeline from Siberia to Western Europe. Initially begun in 1981/1982, this pipeline has been substantially financed by investments in pipe and oil/gas drilling equipment and services from West Germany, France, Italy, and the Netherlands, all of whom have negotiated to be repaid substantially in natural gas. A Norwegian oil serve company (Golan-nor) and a Finnish shipbuilder (Oy Waertsilae) negotiated with the Soviets in 1987 and 1988 to lease them oil-production service vessels in return for oil. The transaction is valued at more than $200 million. The Norwegian company would own two-thirds of the barter project and the Finnish company one-third.

A 1984 sale that the U.S. company, Pepsico, made to the Soviet Union also has attracted a lot of attention in the press. In return for selling some $1 billion of soft drink extract and equipment into the country, the company agreed to export a similar value of Russian vodka out of the country. It had made smaller arrangements like this before.

Among the several transactions listed by Verzariu,[12] Philip Morris countertraded tobacco production machinery for tobacco in 1978. Mitsubishi of Japan traded a ground pulp factory worth $5.5 million and took back production in 1976. Backed by export credit in 1977, Krupp-Koppers of West Germany built a chemical plant worth $125 million and received raw cotton as a partial countertrade in return.

On a smaller scale, the Soviets have attempted to use diamonds from their large stockpiles to buy consumer products from the West. Because of problems regarding quality, the Soviets have been less successful in seeking to countertrade their manufactured products for other goods from the West. Several Eastern Europeans said that although they regard the Soviet Union as a continuing source of raw materials, occasionally the Eastern Bloc countertraded for Soviet-built commercial aircraft or for a Soviet-designed turnkey factory.

In summary, Soviet trade with Eastern Europe is under bilateral clearing agreements. Most of the Soviet countertrade with the West is on a counterpurchase basis directly with companies rather than on a government-to-government basis. In trade with the West the Soviets have emphasized the export of commodities, raw materials including ore, natural gas, and of course vodka. Obviously because of tensions with the West, there have been few opportunities for offsets calling for technology transfer and co-production. Depending on the ebb and flow of tensions, this could change. At least one major U.S. company, Westinghouse, began talks with the Soviets in 1987 about licensing some nonstrategic technology as part of a countertrade if approvals can be granted by the Commerce Department.

POLAND

The foreign trading organizations (FTOs) in Poland appear to be relatively powerful, and have some hard currency resources and financing in addition to strong trading and distribution networks outside of Poland. The FTO is well positioned in many areas including machinery, heavy equipment, and consumer products. One FTO, Torimex, has diverse capability but specializes in retail trading and in exchanges between department stores; another, Bumar, trades in heavy equipment. Polish officials pointed out that some of the independence and flexibility of the FTOs is owed to their not being entirely and directly state-owned. The state might own approximately 51 percent with the remaining portions owned by the state-sponsored corporations. Poland also has a private sector operating within the more dominant state-owned company environment.

The countertrading between Poland and the United States has been significant. In 1978, Occidental Petroleum agreed to countertrade one million tons of Florida phosphate for 500,000 tons of Polish sulfur per year. The contract is for 20 years. Squibb has countertraded antibiotics equipment and taken back pharmaceutical items. There are several examples of U.S.–Polish countertrade both in the sense of counterpurchase and in taking back finished products as payment. Gabriel Wujek, a Polish diplomat in New York, told the story of how a Polish manufacturing company used countertrade to resolve its financial trouble during the economic crisis of the 1980s. The company shipped men's suits to a U.S. retailer for years. Then production had to stop because the Polish company ran out of money to buy buttons and lining. The U.S. company agreed to provide these items and to be repaid through a discount on the additional suits it purchased. Wujek stressed that such financial support could only have happened because of the "good relationship with the U.S. retailer." Singer once used a similar structure to purchase sewing machines in Poland.

When a barter transaction takes place, it is based on an exchange formula. A European retailer agreed to swap 2,000 units of pantyhose against 1,000 units of Polish linen. In a

1983 triangular barter arrangement, a U.S. company was paid in TV sets for chemicals it traded to Poland, finally receiving hard currency only when it sold the TV sets to Turkey.

The popularity of Poland in the United States appears to create a special climate where U.S. firms (perhaps more actively and creatively than in the rest of Eastern Europe) accommodate Polish needs by supporting their sales with countertrade.

HUNGARY

Hungary does not officially require countertrade when trading with the West, but a lot of countertrade happens anyway because of the nonconvertible currency situation. When it happens, countertrade is transacted on a case-by-case basis, for example, in noncash exchanges of consumer goods between Budapest and retailers in Frankfurt and Vienna. The Hungarian Rubber Company exchanged axles with General Motors, International Harvester, and Eaton Corporation, and took back agricultural machinery in return. Endre Juhasz, the Hungarian commercial counselor to the United States, explained that in countertrade with the West "there is no official legislation, no encouragement, no discouragement; it is considered a company matter." He said that the 200 Hungarian companies engaged in significant foreign trade have purchased Western products for cash and that countertrade with the West is somewhat unusual. Hungarian companies appear to play a greater role in negotiating their contracts than, say, their counterparts in Poland where domestic trading companies have greater importance. A Hungarian trader categorically stated that his government does not conclude contracts, even with the Soviet Union:

"The actual trading is carried out by the companies and only the framework is between countries."

In its overall framework, the Hungarian trading system is consistent with those of other Eastern European countries. There are government-to-government trade agreements including yearly quotas based in "clearing rubles"; the balancing among Eastern Bloc countries may take longer than a year as the flows of export goods are adjusted on a credit basis. The Soviets provide Hungary with oil, energy products, raw materials, and commercial aircraft among other items. Hungary exports such products as truck and tractor axles, machinery, buses, engines, air conditioners, rubber tires, tubes, shoes, textiles, and various agricultural products.

CZECHOSLOVAKIA

Czechoslovakia permits countertrade as a legitimate means of carrying on business with the West and of course within the Eastern Bloc. In reality, there have been few exchanges with the West, because much of the countertrade is worked out through the system of bilateral agreements with the Soviets, Eastern Europe, and Asian countries (e.g., India). Czechoslovakian companies have countertraded textiles, shoes, glass, machine tools, mopeds, and tires within the East European system. Partly because of the relatively high duties in the United States, Czechoslovakia has been less successful in trading with U.S. companies.

EAST GERMANY

East Germany's countertrade policy applies counterpurchase requirements to the larger transactions and also requires importers working through the FTOs to link their trading to existing exports (e.g., in the case of Indonesia). The East Germans basically post announcements of what they want to buy and sell. A company wishing to sell into East Germany must have a special license and must link its sale to a corresponding East German export. According to a West German trade official, the process of linking the two trades is facilitated by East Germany's published list of purchases and sales. All a company has to do is find an export that has not been "claimed" by some other company. If the export is not available, the importer must generate it.

Because of a common border, language, and culture, East Germany has a major trading relationship with West Germany. Therefore, countertrading between the two is frequent. East Germany's imports from West Germany include cars, machines, and machine tools, while its exports include garments, cameras, agricultural products, and raw materials such as coal. The clearing currency accounting is negotiated between the West German Bundesbank and the East German central bank. In this system, East and West German currencies are pegged at an equivalent exchange rate. There are renegotiations every few months to keep the system roughly in balance by adjusting trade flows. U.S. trade with East Germany is often carried out through the established West German networks where numerous trading and manufacturing companies have developed a thriving East–West trade.

BULGARIA

Bulgaria's economic problems have forced it to countertrade with the West, although the level of these transactions is low. To countertrade with Bulgaria, a U.S. company must typically work its transaction through the Ministry of Foreign Trade as well as the FTOs, which as in several other East European countries are specialized according to products. For example, one FTO, Chemimport, deals with chemicals; another, Pharmachim, with pharmaceutical products. Dow Chemical arranged a barter transaction through Chemimport. Spas Alakoff, the commercial counselor, explained the structure of a turnkey project where the Japanese built a polypropylene plant in Bulgaria and took back product as payment.

Bulgaria's trading relations with the West are not well developed. The Soviet Union remains its major trading partner on the bilateral clearing basis. It provides Bulgaria with raw materials as well as turnkey projects and commercial aircraft. The Bulgarians sell the Soviets processed food, fruit, wine, liquor, and chemicals.

One European executive recalled painful memories of a barter transaction that was marred by a quality problem, underscoring a risk that must be carefully evaluated in any countertrade. His firm traded machinery into Bulgaria through a Swiss trading company and accepted oil for repayment, thinking it got a good deal because oil is usually sold for cash with relative ease. However, the executive complained that "the oil turned out to be a very low grade and was not so easy to sell off."

RUMANIA

Like the other Eastern European countries, Rumania exports through FTOs such as Comfx (clothing, fabrics), Romano Export (textiles), and Romisit (glass). Rumania has a powerful Ministry of Foreign Trade and an aggressive commercial section based in New York to promote U.S. trade. One

Rumanian company, Universal Tractors, has actively used its sales of tractors into the U.S. market to support, through countertrade, other exports into Rumania.

Perhaps the most celebrated countertrade transaction between a U.S. company and Rumania began with the country's liquidity crisis in 1981. In the late 1970s, General Electric (GE) contracted to sell a $150 million turbine generator project supported by a loan from the U.S. Export-Import Bank (Eximbank). When Rumania's credit situation worsened, Eximbank revoked the loan, leaving GE with a production schedule to meet. There were two choices for GE, take the loss by stopping work or find an alternative. The option GE chose was to initiate a barter relationship, taking out Rumanian products such as chemicals, metals, steel, rebar, and nails to generate cash for the project. The GE power generating division went ahead and completed the project while the GE Trading Company took the barter obligation on a credit basis, accepting Rumanian products and finding buyers for them long after the project was completed. GE was so successful in saving the project that its efforts became the subject of a Harvard Business School case study. When I talked to Michael Cosgrove of the GE Trading Company about the ongoing barter obligation in August 1987, he said he was just $3 million short of fulfilling the commitment, and finished in a matter of months.

Rumania's countertrading is active with the Eastern Bloc and Soviet Union under the clearing currency system. Like Yugoslavia, Rumania appears to be relatively well organized for trade, more open to the West, and at times more willing to mix cash and barter even within Eastern Europe. The Yugoslav commercial attaché, a former manager of a petrochemical complex in Pancevo, near Belgrade, recalled a long-term contract with Rumania to supply propylene, ethylene, and other petrochemicals for a combination of hard currency and "clearing currency." Rumania balanced the transaction with a combination of oil, salt, and chemicals including diammonium phosphate.

SUMMARY

There are clearly informal obstacles to trade between U.S. companies and Eastern Europe. Despite notable Japanese and U.S. exceptions, European corporations and trading companies dominate the trade and orient it toward Western Europe with whom traditional trading networks are well organized and are enhanced by geography. Countertrade is probably hindered with the United States and even Western Europe by the absence of government-to-government "clearing account" or other framework agreements that are the basis of so much trade within Eastern Europe. Finland, which imports 90 percent of its oil from the Soviet Union, overcame this problem by signing up a long-term framework agreement with the Soviets. The trade flows are recorded through an evidence account in the Bank of Finland, as the two countries attempt to balance their trading each year. India has a similar agreement with the Soviet Union.

Security concerns also hinder potential U.S. trading with, among others, the Soviet Union, East Germany, and Bulgaria. If a U.S. company seeks to bring countertraded products back into the United States, traditional trade barriers (e.g., generally higher duties for Eastern Europe's products) become relevant.

As in the People's Republic of China, great opportunities exist where East European countries are willing to sign large raw materials agreements and to encourage investment in turnkey products that can be paid for by taking back product.

Also, the East Europeans have shown a willingness to trade by establishing active trade missions in New York, unlike several OPEC nations for example, and are aggressively seeking to expand into the U.S. market.

In the absence of bilateral trading arrangements, the successful U.S. company establishes a pattern in its countertrading with Eastern Europe. It develops the expertise to market East European products through its own resources or by developing relations with the appropriate trading company, and it builds a relationship through patient, sustaining negotiations with its trading partner.

Chapter Thirteen

Tribal Barter

"In order to trade, man must first lay down his spear."
—MARCEL MAUSS, *The Gift*, 1925

A NEW IMPORTANCE

Countertrade is not a single technique but an approach to doing business and thinking about business that raises the balancing of relationships to a new importance. It is in this crucial sense that countertrade resembles so-called tribal barter. Not too many years ago, a seller and a buyer made a deal when a sufficient amount of money was put on the table to motivate a seller to part with his goods. There was a feeling of reciprocity especially if both parties felt they got a fair deal. While this time-honored tradition continues for basic retail items such as food and consumer products, the payment of mere cash is no longer considered fair or reciprocal by many buyers for their larger purchases of military systems and other high-tech items like telecommunications equipment and commercial aircraft.

Why is this so? The discussion of military offsets provided a number of answers. Foreign exchange in an era of higher oil prices has become too precious and hard to get. Sellers must now provide ways for the buyer to get back all or part of a buyer's foreign exchange spent in a sale. They must also help the buyer recover from the technical losses suffered by domestic industry when they lose a contract to a foreign importer. Jobs are lost and need to be restored. If the imported military or high-tech system is large enough, political damage can occur and needs to be repaired. The seller who takes care of these issues well is far more likely to build a long-term relationship than one who is lucky enough to sell products merely for cash, without additional commitments. The Japanese, for example, are famous for the careful, long-term nurturing of business relationships. This is one fundamental reason for their success in international trade.

BUILDING AND MAINTAINING RELATIONSHIPS

Offset and countertrade, for better or worse, do place more value on the building and maintaining of relationships. Indeed, they place more value on reciprocity. In this sense, I began to wonder about something fundamental here, happening at a structural level, calling for a whole series, perhaps a never-ending series, of reciprocal activities when trading is seen by purchasing countries in more life-or-death terms. I began to think of these large corporate countertrade sales in the way that goods are traded and eligible women and men are married in tribal society. Suddenly relationships become more important and even the pure symbolism of exchange for its own sake becomes more significant in certain cases. Certainly, there must be such symbolism somewhere, in the Indonesian system for example, when countertrading "with mirrors" adds little economic value to the process but is viewed by the government as an edifying, helpful process. The practice of the Japanese business executive of calling on clients frequently, taking them out to dinner, and giving them thoughtful gifts is all part of the supposedly "noneconomic," symbolic aspects of maintaining business relationships. I feel there are similarities between corporate countertrade and tribal barter. Perhaps some probing into the latter would turn up even more revealing fundamentals.

As a businessman trained in anthropology, I initially wanted to examine the anthropological literature in hopes of showing how countertrade among companies and nations may have evolved from tribal barter. As will be seen in this chapter, such an exercise turned out to be a pointless endeavor because many tribal peoples appear to place a far greater importance on maintaining and ultimately balancing relationships than on making a profit through their exchange. In a way, corporate barter and countertrade seem to be a modern creation, based on a misunderstanding about how tribal barter really works. If modern trading among nations emulated the patterns of tribal societies, it would be difficult for some countries to have huge trade surpluses and others to have huge deficits. However, on a more narrow level modern counterpurchase, offset, and barter do seek to correct some of these imbalances.

In the anthropological literature there are numerous colorful examples of exchange among the tribal people, such as the Nuer of southern Sudan in East Africa and the Mandinka of Senegal and Gambia in West Africa, where various forms of barter including marriage are a way of building relationships. The relationship is almost more important than the economic value of the goods exchanged. The relationship *is* the economic value. The goods and the relationship cannot be easily separated.

The anthropological literature demonstrates very vividly the deep human need, cutting across all levels of economic development, for balancing and maintaining relationships over a long time in order to trade and exchange goods successfully. The capacity of modern countertrade to benefit from balancing and maintaining relationships over time is one of its great appeals, providing an important lesson for business generally.

BARTER MISUNDERSTOOD

Yet barter is still very much a misunderstood concept in the United States, where it is treated as a means of last resort, a desperation measure to close a sale when nothing else will work. It has a negative connotation drawn from perhaps the most famous barter deal of all time: the purchase of Manhattan Island by Dutch traders for a few dollars' worth of colored glass beads. Prejudiced by humorous examples like this one, Americans have incorrectly come to think of barter as a "lower" form of trading. They believe it is for people with no civilization and without the sophistication to understand money, who swap products as a way of getting what they want. The deal is signed with an "Ugh!" and a handshake, and someone is taken to the cleaners because of the vast imbalance in the value of the products swapped.

Among tribal peoples, the need to exchange gifts and products emerges as a fundamental of human existence. Exchange does not merely have an economic importance to these peoples, but a "total" importance relevant to all aspects of their lives, from marriage to the creation of alliances necessary for tribal self-defense. Above all, the process of exchange, properly carried out according to accepted customs, maintains or cultivates relationships among groups of people. Exchange or trade would not be possible except for "good relations."

The most famous anthropological book on barter was written by a French sociologist, Marcel Mauss, for the journal *Année Sociologique* in Paris in 1925. This essay, called simply *The Gift* in English translation, has become a classic of the 20th century, oddly enough not because of its insights into the fundamentals of trade.[13] Instead, *The Gift* is credited with inspiring modern structuralism, a movement that has become a major force in psychology, literary criticism, linguistics, and anthropology.

GIFT-GIVING

Mauss wrote that what tribal peoples "exchange is not exclusively goods and wealth, real and personal property, and things of economic value. They exchange rather courtesies, entertainments, ritual, military assistance, women, children, dances, and feasts; and fairs in which the market is but one element and the circulation of wealth but one part of a wide and enduring contract" (see Ref. 13, p. 3). Mauss saw in these gifts and "counter-gifts" a whole new system of "total prestations" or gift-giving, with formal rules that were strictly obligatory and for which the failure to comply often meant war. Mauss's use of the French term "counter-gifts" is suggestive of, and perhaps the earliest use of, the very term *countertrade*. We can draw from Mauss's observations certain fundamentals relevant to contemporary society. It is easy to understand the sensitivity of a modern government over the failure of a company to live up to an offset or countertrade obligation; the strong, emotional responses of government officials sometimes transcend economies and reach the level of values, status, and courtesy so typical of the peoples documented by anthropologists.

Crucially, Mauss believed gifts were not voluntary but were given and repaid under obligation, a kind of moral compulsion to repay. He observed that trading is transacted among identifiable, corporate "groups, and not individuals, which carry on exchange, make contracts, and are bound by obligations" (see Ref. 13, p. 3). In examining the Maoris of New Zealand, Mauss concluded that things given, called *taonga*, have a value greater than themselves, a spirit called *hau*. The *hau* of the gift forces the recipient to pass it on and return it ultimately to the initial giver. The giver is giving a part of himself, something representative of himself. The personality and ego of the gift-giver are wrapped up in the gift. Mauss concluded that to break the cycle by failure to give a gift is dangerous, causing a loss of face.

The circulatory nature of gift-giving is perhaps best illustrated by the *kula* system of trading among the Trobriand Islanders in the Western Pacific. *Kula* literally means "ring" in the Trobriand language. It was a system of exchange between recognized partners in different villages, involving finely cut armshells worn by men and necklaces worn by women. These items could not be kept and had to be passed on. Their value was seen in terms of the overall *kula* with the best items having long histories and important associations. Ritual expeditions to exchange these items often covered great distances between the islands and helped create alliances, reducing tensions. Mauss observed this and other examples and concluded dramatically that Trobriand barter did not create simply a gift received but "a pledge and a loan, an object sold and an object bought, a deposit, a mandate, a trust . . . given only on the condition that it will be used on behalf of, or transmitted to a third person" (see Ref. 13, p. 22).

Mauss arrived at the conclusion that barter as a simple economic exchange of products did not exist among tribal peoples and was not a relevant concept to them. In Mauss's system of "gifts and return gifts," the themes of credit and honor are of paramount importance, assuring that gifts would be returned. He saw barter as well as purchase and sale almost as Western inventions derived from these tribal systems of gift-giving (see Ref. 13, p. 35). Mauss concluded by viewing trade, in which products are exchanged on a gift-giving basis, as the opposite of war. The good relations created by trading are far more important than the economic nature of the goods exchanged, making it difficult to fight.

MARRIAGE SYSTEM

In another classic, if controversial, work of anthropology, Claude Levi-Strauss took Mauss's theme of exchange and gift-giving and applied it to marriage, in particular to a tendency among certain tribal peoples to marry their cousins.[14] Levi-Strauss' arguments, still hotly debated, that structural integration in tribal groups results from marriage and the accompanying exchanges of goods suggest to me the reciprocal, almost integrative aspects of countertrade. Perhaps I am giving Levi-Strauss too much credit, but at least in marriage one can understand the integrative aspects of exchange more directly than in the exchange of trade goods, although integration nevertheless occurs here also.

He begins with the concept that "to trade" means "to make peace with" and points out one tribal language where the same verb in fact means both. He argues that the most important form of exchange in primitive societies involves not simply material objects and value, but the acquisition of women in marriage. "For the woman herself is nothing other than one of these gifts, the supreme gift among those that can only be obtained in the form of reciprocal gifts." Levi-Strauss argues that a certain type of marriage system among tribal peoples is best at creating social integration because daughters are exchanged in the same circulating direction across several generations. He says that this system, in which sons try to marry their maternal uncles' daughters, is best because it creates a more inclusive longer cycle of alliances than another type of marriage, with the paternal uncles' daughters, which creates a shorter cycle of alliances. Perhaps what Levi-Strauss describes is a long-term structural basis for trading, deriving from a human need for integration that is consistent and understandable.

The creation of alliances by marriage provides one of the most interesting trading institutions among tribal people—namely, the bridewealth. Bridewealth is really a form of countertrade, compensating the wife's family for the loss of economic services. Among the Kedang people of Indonesia bridewealth gifts, including required tusks or gongs, take many decades to be paid, with the obligation often taken care of by children or grandchildren.[15] The Nuer of the southern Sudan, famous for raising cattle, have in the past required a small herd to be given for a new bride. Among the Mandinko in West Africa, gift-giving begins soon after infant daughters are betrothed and continues not only through marriage but with the bearing of children. The gifts most often include cash and a contribution of goats or sheep.[16] Examples such as these suggest that the bridewealth and the relationship its payment symbolizes are compensation for the loss of something very precious. Bridewealth, as Levi-Strauss observes, "has less to do with sexual rights . . . than with the permanent loss of the wife and her offspring" (see Ref. 14, p. 260).

What is key here is the importance tribal people place on using their trading or gift-giving as a means to facilitate and validate relationships among groups of people.

For the Yanomamo in the Amazon jungle, this principle has been a matter of life and death. They are trading to create excuses for repetitive visits and feasting as a way of maintaining stable alliances among villages. Napoleon Chagnon observed during his fieldwork that Yanomamo villages not allied often engaged in bitter raiding and warfare leading to fatalities.[17]

MODERN BARTER IS HERE TO STAY

Mauss and Levi-Strauss, who contrasted trading and warfare, might find at least one irony in some of the huge countertrade transactions being put together today. The largest and best-known examples are the military offsets meant to support major international weapons sales. While the scale and motives of these tribal and corporate transactions vastly differ, one similarity is clear: There must be reciprocity. As we have seen, very few exporters of weapons or even turnkey projects will walk away from their sale with cash alone. They must also promise to transfer technology, to subcontract components, to jointly invest in industries, or to export the purchasing country's products to third markets. Modern barter in the narrow economic sense, stripped of its symbolism and placed in a total system of values, is not something a tribal people could have easily invented, but it appears here to stay.

SUMMARY

Corporate countertrade is most like tribal barter when it builds a long-term relationship and creates a series of reciprocal activities in military offsets, for example. The purchasing of a single system of F-16s in Turkey is structured with the Foreign Military Sales (FMS) loan repayment spread out over a period of some ten years. Against this flow of cash payments, General Dynamics sees to it that a series of investment and trading activity occurs. This sort of countertrade can be integrative, like a series of marriages between two extended families. It creates a whole series of transactions and events where the two sides or groups have to deal with each other amicably, peacefully, for the process to keep going. This integrative potential of trading is highlighted in Mauss's observation that "in order to trade, man must first lay down his spear."

The importance of the purchase to the buyer is so great that the need to reciprocate is almost forced by the large nature of the transaction. The buying country is sensitive to losses of foreign exchange, jobs, and technology. The product purchased is not adequate compensation in the eyes of the buyer, who demands the additional compensating activity under the offset. The political nature of large military purchases is especially acute, and the offset, while dealing with economic and technological compensation, also provides the buyer with important symbolic values to use in domestic debates.

Ironically, corporate countertrade is less like tribal barter the closer the transaction comes to being pure barter in the sense of swapping one good for another. This is because corporate barter succeeds best when it is highly focused. The less complicated a corporate barter is, the better. The economic need for the transaction is also more focused than offset where other technology and job-related issues play a greater role. In such an environment, speed is of the essence, whereas in tribal barter the reciprocity and its supporting transactions are never-ending. Finishing transactions more quickly means less time exists for things to go wrong. There is little room in the focused pressure of the corporate barter for symbolic value to play an important role, although a role does nevertheless exist.

Even the most focused barter is typically so difficult to put together that it requires relationships and goodwill of unusual proportions. Both sides have to want very much for the transaction to happen with perhaps even more determination than would be required in a cash-only sale. All kinds of corporate countertrade, even barter, keep coming back to "the relationship," whose importance in tribal transactions helps to provide an idiom for understanding the crucial nature of this concept.

Corporate countertrade differs most from tribal barter because economics and profitability take precedence over everything else including ultimately even the relationship. Tribal groups, on the other hand, seem to be striving for a greater sense of balance at all levels from the symbolic to the economic, and this takes precedence over everything else.

Chapter Fourteen

Corporate Tactics

*"If you don't integrate everything
you are doing all over the world,
and extract offset value from it,
you're missing a lot of gimmies
that you don't have to pay for."*
—PAT HALL, Vice President and Director,
Rockwell International Trading Company

DIFFERING APPROACHES

There is no standard model for the countertrade structure within large U.S. companies, and no typical strategy for approaching countertrade and offset. Most larger U.S. companies have at least some capacity to deal with the issue, especially if they export significantly in either defense or nondefense areas. The approaches range from General Dynamics (GD), which has a small unincorporated unit of about ten people and does not do any trading, to General Electric (GE) Trading Company with 85 people with a preference for trading. Despite differing approaches, several larger U.S. companies deal with offset and countertrade very effectively.

ROCKWELL INTERNATIONAL

Rockwell International Trading Company is a small group of five people formally incorporated as a Delaware Corporation. It was set up to assist the operating divisions with negotiating and structuring the offset or countertrade transaction and with implementing it afterward. Rockwell is the vehicle for signing the offset or countertrade obligation but, unlike GE, usually does no trading for its own account. If trading is needed, a trading company is brought in to take the products. Any commission obtained goes into the operating division's price for the initial sale. This was the approach used in Rockwell's printing press transaction with Zimbabwe (see Chapter 7).

Rockwell's style of satisfying offset obligations, which differs from GD's investment approach, is to direct its procurement or sourcing of subassemblies and components to its offset target countries. Until recently, Rockwell has been able to fulfill 75–80 percent of its indirect offset requirements in this manner, representing some $450–500 million in completed obligations. The procurement approach is built off one of Rockwell's great strengths, a worldwide diversification that is stronger on the nondefense side, for example, than that of GD. Thus, Rockwell's automotive brake investment in Turkey was not needed for any Rockwell offset obligations there and could be applied to GD's F-16 obligation. Rockwell's procurement strategy is also dictated by the smaller scale of its transactions, resulting from the subcontracting role it plays in most defense sales. Its offsets are typically in the $10–20 million range in support of defense exports in the areas of marine systems, missiles, and avionics components.

Pat Hall of Rockwell (see Chapter 7) stressed that the key factors for the success of his strategy are *total integration* and *flexibility* in his procurement (sourcing or purchasing). His staff closely monitors sourcing worldwide so that purchases can be matched with offset commitments anywhere. (The defense contractor, Raytheon in Lexington, Massachusetts, uses a similar approach through its procurement office.)

In one significant case, Rockwell was recently bidding on a hotly contested $500 million contract for the combat systems integration for six Australian submarines. The requirements under the Australian industry involvement program were extremely heavy, so heavy in fact that Rockwell "simply offered to move this whole effort to Australia and make it an Australian program with some small amount of imports." Rockwell recently won the transaction by making good on its offer to move construction and systems integration work to Australia, establishing virtually the entire program as the offset. But the company did not stop there. It will attempt to use the subcontract requirements for the

Australian program to comply with offset commitments elsewhere in the world. This was done to fulfill Rockwell's prior subcontracting commitment to Boeing, calling for Rockwell's participation in Boeing's 130 percent offset for its recent AWACs sale to both the United Kingdom and France.

GENERAL DYNAMICS

Like Boeing, General Dynamics (GD) as a prime contractor finds itself confronted with large offset commitments and must seek help from its subcontractors to make headway. GD now routinely signs agreements with all its subcontractors, requiring them to assist with offset if they procure components in a country and are unable to use that sourcing to fulfill their own commitment somewhere. For example, GD got help from Rockwell in Turkey with the brake investment mentioned above because it was already a supplier to GD. Rockwell was an electronics subcontractor for GD's M-1 tank. In the sale of F-16s to Singapore GD got some credit for offset there through an independent investment by United Technologies Corporation, another one of its many subcontractors.

GD's strategy emphasizing subcontractors and its commitment to investment are likely to continue as important methods for fulfilling indirect offset obligations. In a recent sale of 40 F-16s to Greece, GD has again proposed an investment strategy and is relying on principal subcontractors to absorb the cost. The subcontractors, GE (21.3%) and Westinghouse (13%), have agreed to co-invest with GD (65.7%) a total of $50 million in the Hellenic Business Development and Investment Company as the centerpiece of the offset proposal. The purpose of the Hellenic Company will be to invest throughout Greece in companies whose capacity to export will generate foreign exchange. Once the $50 million total has been invested, a decision will be made on whether to keep the company going.

GENERAL ELECTRIC

The General Electric Trading Company was initially established in 1982 as a profit center but has taken on a "problem-solving" role in the view of Michael Cosgrove, the savvy vice president of countertrade and barter who was a founding member of the company. The volume of trading has stabilized at almost $200 million per year. GE Trading has about 20 people assigned to countertrade negotiations and management, 40 traders, and 20 financial and clerical people. It also has small offices in Turkey, Spain, South Korea, and Rumania. The first three offices are to develop and support military offset programs: for GD in Turkey, for McDonnell-Douglas in Spain, and for South Korea generally because offset programs have become commonplace there in the last three years. Now that the parent corporation GE has acquired RCA, which has extensive defense contracts, GE Trading is likely to pick up responsibility for even more offset commitments.

Because GE is well organized to handle trading, it has a natural orientation to use these skills in countertrade, even to support military offsets. As a subcontractor for the engines, GE supports the McDonnell-Douglas F-18 offset in Spain exclusively with the trading of chemicals and metals including steel rebar and aluminum. GE pursued two other transactions in Spain where trading was required. GE's recent transactions also emphasize trading. The parent company sold locomotives to a mining company in Gabon, Africa, and GE Trading agreed to take back ferromanganese. GE sold turbines to a Chinese province for a combination of cash and products. Rumania negotiated to continue acquiring plant and equipment through the existing countertrading arrangement with GE (discussed in Chapter 12) that helped to pay for the power generator plant. However, if Congress removes Rumania's most-favored-nation status, duties would rise on exports coming to the United States, making the cost of the transaction prohibitive.

Not all of GE's transactions will involve trading. South Korea is insisting on technology transfers and on the kind of direct offsets that are normally carried out through corporate procurement programs. Nevertheless, Michael Cosgrove sees a growth of infrastructure projects in Third World countries and believes that GE Trading will be well positioned to handle the countertrade that will be required to facilitate many of these projects.

WESTINGHOUSE

Westinghouse, like Rockwell, has participated in many of its offset obligations because of its role as a subcontractor. Chuck Martin, the director of international licensing and countertrade at Westinghouse, described a conservative approach where his company prefers to be drawn into countertrade transactions and does not initiate them. The countertrade staff consists of three people in its corporate headquarters in Pittsburgh and one to two people in the headquarters for the Westinghouse Defense Group in Baltimore, Maryland (a major part of the corporation). The defense countertrade unit is responsible for about 95 percent of the military offsets but receives guidance from the countertrade staff in Pittsburgh. Martin described his system as a low-cost approach in which outside help is brought in frequently. He has worked with consultants to help his unit design countertrade strategies in a country such as China and with trading companies to trade products received through countertrade arrangements. In the previously mentioned coffee/generator swap in Latin America, a trading company was called in to take the coffee. Martin summed up his approach by saying: "We have creative, solid countertrade experience around the world, but as other companies decided to hire larger countertrade staffs, we have stayed small."

A barter-type countertrade transaction put together by Westinghouse Defense (Baltimore) illustrates this approach of relying on outside help. The unit recently negotiated the sale of an air defense radar system worth $100 million to the Kingdom of Jordan. An additional $15 million was for site preparation.

Jordan found itself in a situation similar to Turkey's. Foreign Military Sales (FMS) funds had been exhausted for the country. Commercial banks were unwilling to take on Jordanian risk for the number of years required to finance this transaction. As so often happens, commercial bank terms were unacceptable and government financing was unavailable. Westinghouse turned to trading companies for help.

Lor-West Trading in Bermuda structured the transaction based on trading assistance from the giant Japanese trading company, Mitsubishi. Lor-West is 20 percent owned by Westinghouse and 80 percent owned by Lorad Company of Bermuda, a wholly owned subsidiary of the Wraxall Group in the United Kingdom. The Group's Douglas Leese, based in the United Kingdom, has responsibility for the subsidiaries in Bermuda and also helped to put the sale together. Westinghouse Defense served as a subcontractor, with Lor-West in the prime contractor role.

Mitsubishi sells phosphate, offered to it by Jordan, to its customer base around the world. The nature of Mitsubishi's payment guarantees to Westinghouse is confidential and cannot be disclosed. The foreign exchange proceeds from the phosphate sales are remitted from Mitsubishi back to a special account in the central bank of Jordan. There are separate contracts between Lor-West and Mitsubishi, Mitsubishi and the central bank, and the central bank and Lor-West, setting up payment procedures. The central bank has issued an unconfirmed letter of credit to Lor-West. As payments for the air defense system are required they are paid automatically through the letter of credit out of an escrow account in a Chase Manhattan bank in the United Kingdom's Channel Islands. The offshore payment mechanism, outside of Jordan, provides additional assurances to Lor-West and Westinghouse that funds will be transferred smoothly as the delivery schedule for the radar is met.

Mitsubishi began the phosphate trading in June 1985 and by December 1987 had generated $70 million for the transaction, more than two-thirds of the requirement. Its goal is to collect and generate money faster than Westinghouse can spend it, although lately Mitsubishi has been concerned with the quality of some of the phosphate.

The large trading company with an established network is in a much better position to structure this type of transaction than a money center bank that has a small, recently established trading subsidiary. The large trading company's established orientation toward commodities can serve it well. Hopefully, more of these transactions can be designed where bank financing is not available. In this sense, the Jordanian case is an important model.

McDONNELL-DOUGLAS

Compared with Westinghouse, McDonnell-Douglas has a larger, decentralized countertrade organization designed to serve each of the five major corporate divisions, McDonnell-Douglas Aircraft Corporation (the defense aircraft company), Douglas Aircraft (the commercial aircraft company), the Information Systems Group, Astronautics, and the helicopter company. There are centralized countertrade departments and supporting staff in each of the five divisions all reporting to a single coordinator, Jim Brady, at corporate headquarters in St. Louis, Missouri. Douglas Aircraft has 20 people in a countertrade unit reporting to Phil Rowberg at Douglas headquarters in Long Beach, California.

Normally, the commercial aircraft business does not run into the large offsets characteristic of defense exporting. Rowberg recalled that countertrade has never been required to support McDonnell-Douglas sales in Africa or Latin America. Unlike military offsets, countertrade percentages when required for commercial aircraft are much smaller than 100 percent of sales value. If the purchasing airline does buy aircraft through countertrade, it usually makes a cash payment and then barters the products over time to generate enough cash to reach the purchase price. Yugoslavia has used this approach with McDonnell-Douglas since the late 1960s, including the recent purchase of DC-10s. To support these countertrade commitments, a Yugoslavian foreign trade organization (FTO) maintains an office at Douglas headquarters to manage the selling, not just of its famous hams (known to all students of countertrade history), but some 30–40 other products. Douglas has arranged for the FTO staff to truck the ham to plant cafeterias and to factory locations for sale directly to employees at designated times of the year including Christmas.

Rowberg explained that while Douglas has formed a co-production venture in China to assemble aircraft and to manufacture components, the company has a preference for trading products or using sourcing to fulfill its countertrade requirements. Douglas has avoided hiring trading companies and uses its own countertrade expertise in working directly with the purchasing country.

BOEING

Boeing is another aircraft company faced with growing demands for offsets by foreign countries, both for its defense sales and even for its exports of commercial aircraft, which make a significant contribution to overall U.S. exports of manufactured goods. At one level, Boeing has an outspoken, highly visible policy of doing everything possible to avoid signing up offset obligations. Boeing generally treats countertrade as a tactic of last resort.

On another level, Boeing has increasingly been forced in stiff make-or-break competitions to become very good at designing offset packages in order to win sales. On the defense side, as discussed in Chapter 4, Boeing had to offer 130 percent offset to win the AWACS sale in the United Kingdom as well as in France. Like GD, Boeing tries to get help for satisfying offset obligations from its subcontractors. Boeing can also use its tremendous sourcing (procurement) capability worldwide, both in defense and for its large commercial aircraft operation, to help meet these offset demands. It is in this latter area that U.S. subcontractors could see their sales eroded as the prime contractor is forced to shift more and more subcontracting to countries such as France and the United Kingdom to satisfy the large offset obligations in these countries. Boeing, however, insists with credibility that such products must meet industry standards both for price and for technical specifications.

In the commercial aircraft area, Boeing is encountering offset in countries where it did not exist previously. Using a loophole in the General Agreement on Tariffs and Trade (GATT), Greece is trying to collect 60 percent offset for a fleet of 767s being sold to it. Under the GATT agreement on commercial aircraft it is forbidden for a signatory nation (of GATT) or a member of the European Economic Community (EEC) to require offset in this area. Greece is a member of the EEC but has not signed the GATT. Boeing is also troubled by a recent offset requirement in Brazil, an old and loyal client country, for 10 percent offset over a ten-year period for new purchases by Varig (Brazil's national airline). Officials at Boeing and the Brazilians are uncertain about how the offset is to be fulfilled. Boeing also has commercial offset agreements with China, Yugoslavia, and Australia. Boeing's agreements with these countries are mostly fulfilled by a combination of sourcing (procuring components) and technology transfer. None of Boeing's commercial aircraft obligations appears to include investment in a particular country or much counterpurchase in the sense of buying or promoting general exports from that country.

Boeing has found that in its own experience sourcing is cheaper than counterpurchase, which usually requires trading companies with commissions. Countertrade initially proposed to Boeing by both Yugoslavia and Pakistan was on a less than satisfactory counterpurchase basis. The company persuaded the countries that sourcing would be in their best interest because it would strengthen certain of their high-tech industries selected to sell components directly into Boeing's plants. In the case of Pakistan, Boeing supported its sourcing with some technology transfer to Precision Electronics

Group (a subsidiary of the Airline PAI) to help Pakistan meet industry standards.

In South Korea, Boeing has pursued an informal countertrade approach, selling it 747 jumbo jets while sourcing both components and raw materials without a formal countertrade commitment. The company has used flexibility by arranging countertrade where it must, and restraint, steering away from measures such as exporting general products where it has not built up staff expertise. Like Westinghouse and Rockwell, Boeing's actual staff of two people in defense and six in commercial is small in the industry among larger companies and is minuscule compared to the corporations like General Electric and General Motors that have set up full trading companies.

OTHER EXAMPLES

There are other examples of what U.S. companies have done to organize for countertrade. Among the many U.S. companies that have set up countertrade units are Lockheed, Northrop, and Combustion Engineering.

In 1979, General Motors (GM) established a major in-house trading company called Motors Trading Corporation. As the largest U.S. exporter, GM felt that a trading company would facilitate sales in countries where countertrade was required. GM is thus the largest U.S. manufacturer to have a formal trading company. Motors Trading has been directly involved in transactions worth hundreds of millions of dollars, ranging from mineral ores to other commodities, manufactured goods, and even grass mats (see Ref. 8, p. 15). Annual trading volume ranges between $100 million and $200 million.

Keeping overhead relatively small, Motors Trading employs 40 people, including a small overseas staff. The trading company takes title to products if necessary, but has also passed this risk-taking measure off to other companies. As one official at Motors said: "We don't run from taking title if necessary. However when you buy a countertrade product for your own account, a letter of credit must be opened with a bank, adding a cost up front of $\frac{1}{2}$ percent to the transaction."

In contrast to Motors Trading's larger size, Monsanto has essentially a one-person trading company, managed by Dan West. Several Monsanto executives based overseas coordinate with West on a dotted line basis, allowing him to carry out transactions worth tens of millions of dollars with minimal overhead. West has a preference for taking title to countertrade goods because it allows him to watch and take possession of the money paid for products, even if only for a short while. He presells every possible product before taking title, to lower his risk and to shorten the time, sometimes to mere minutes, of his actual possession. He has traded a considerable variety of products, including high blood pressure medicine, tin, tuna fish, wooden pallets, orange juice, and shirts.

Both Monsanto Trading and Motors Trading are cost centers set up to provide a service to the corporation and not to serve as profit centers. They facilitate transactions for other profit centers in their overall corporations.

Caterpillar World Trading has a different philosophy. It is organized as an independent subsidiary with the purpose of making a profit while generating incremental sales for Caterpillar. When necessary, it stays in the middle of transactions by taking title. Its goal is thus to facilitate sales of Caterpillar equipment, but unlike many other in-house trading companies, it is held accountable for making a profit while performing this service. Caterpillar also has an innovative "materials management" program, which helps suppliers to Caterpillar to lower their costs by purchasing components from selected countries overseas. In this way, Caterpillar generates countertrade credit, enabling it to sell products into a country such as China, by proving that it has helped generate exports from China with the materials management program. Caterpillar operates its countertrade unit with about 25 people worldwide, with 13 in Peoria, Illinois and the rest in Hong Kong, Geneva, Brussels, and Miami.

Other countertrading companies have been set up on a profit-making basis. In 1983, George Horton and some colleagues left Citibank to found in New York a profit-making countertrade subsidiary of the West German trading company, Metallgesellschaft. Called MG Services, the new company grew to a staff of 50 people before retracting somewhat. It has formed ventures with the investment bank First Boston and other companies. The commodity trading houses of Phibro-Salomon, Continental Grain, and Cargill have all organized modest-sized units to assist companies with countertrade on a profit-making basis. The money center banks entered the business through the Export Trading Company Act in the early 1980s. Many have scaled these export trading companies back somewhat but have found them interesting development vehicles to generate both countertrading business outright and the lucrative financing services that support countertrading by manufacturing companies.

The structure of successful countertrading groups varies considerably in the United States, but the qualities that make them successful remain the same. These include Pat Hall's flexibility and total integration and Cary Viktor's tenacity and creativity.

U.S. corporate strategies vary widely. Even the incidence of countertrade by industry group varies considerably. While countertrade in the offset sense is an active phenomenon in military sales, it now appears to be increasingly used in large purchases of telecommunications and power-generation equipment and commercial aircraft. Exports of engineering and construction services require little countertrade; consumer products need even less. In the counterpurchase area, most exports run into countertrade in the countries of Eastern Europe, Latin America, and elsewhere where it is national policy.

FACING PROBLEMS OF COUNTERTRADE

Relatively few large U.S. companies in manufacturing (General Electric and General Motors being among the exceptions) have set up large, well-financed trading companies with trading capacity running into hundreds of millions of dollars. The majority of other companies that are organized to deal with countertrade approach it with a small, skilled staff.

Here the strategies can be quite different. McDonnell-Douglas and Westinghouse emphasize trading along with procurement and some technology transfer; they rely on outside trading companies to meet their needs. Boeing, Rockwell, and Raytheon, to name a few, stress procurement and technology transfer and avoid trading except where necessary. In the United States, the manufacturers who succeed best at countertrade help themselves, either by trading on their own account or by playing a key role in designing the trading strategy.

Companies looking to provide countertrade service to other companies have had a real struggle. Sears tried for three years, had a change of heart, and stopped. General Electric once tried to provide the service for clients and stopped, concentrating on its own needs. MG Services is cutting back. Many trading companies within the banks have scaled back original expectations, although some, like Bank of America Trading, continue to look for business. U.S. grain and commodity companies are best suited to do countertrade but have yet to emphasize it with perhaps the strategic focus and financial backing required.

Overseas companies appear to have had the best track record, with the large Japanese trading companies playing the greatest service role, and European trading companies including those in West Germany having some success.

The difficulties and stresses in countertrade are forcing it to evolve. There is some trend toward increasing technology transfer and procurement, as well as investment. Cost-benefit analyses place limits on these approaches.

Many companies look increasingly for ways to avoid trading, especially under military offset agreement. The reason for this is quite fundamental. Countries that request trading under military offsets place strong pressure on the selling company to take back less marketable products.

The struggle in all forms of countertrade is for the seller to convince the buyer that the "best" (most marketable) products must be made available, while the seller wants to promote the least-marketable products in sizable quantities.

Critical problems arise for the trading company seeking to enter the offset business for clients. If the trader supports a bid for an offset package, the defense contractor may not be the winner or the purchaser may cancel the bid. A lot of work goes down the drain. If the trader goes after existing obligations, where more success is possible, other problems arise. The agreement has been struck and in some cases whole classes of products are contractually declared ineligible for countertrade. The trader may have to settle for less desirable products, which are not so easy to sell, if he wants any offset business. A further problem is the trader's lack of leverage with an existing offset obligation. There is less flexibility overall. The seller has made a sale and therefore is less willing to pay a commission of greater than 5 percent. The officers who care most about the sale may have moved elsewhere in the company. The buying country is less willing to make exceptions on rules governing export licenses, remittance of foreign exchange, and eligibility of products.

SUMMARY

What the trading company needs to succeed in the counter-trade business is leverage, the ability to mold a sale in one's favor. This is why some of the most profitable counter-trade transactions for a trading company may prove to be not in offsets, but in financial engineering. By financial engineering I mean designing finance packages that somehow mix commodities and financing or guarantees to make a sale go through when both government financing and commercial bank export financing, already dried up in much of the world for terms longer than a year, are simply not available. The ability to finance sales (e.g., General Electric's Rumanian barter and Mitsubishi's Jordanian barter) is an important aspect of countertrade. It is here in the role of financier that the trading company's leverage is strongest and the potential earnings greatest, helping to compensate for the risks.

The best barter transactions manage risk well, by separating financing into pieces conditioned on delivery of products, and by establishing clear criteria for valuation, shipping, delivery, and insurance.

It is possible that where leverage is greatest, the chance for success is underestimated, and the potential for barter financing or commodity-backed financing is relatively untapped. Would the money center banks, in making so many loans to Latin American countries that are now in default, have fared better if the central bank guarantees, as well as nonguaranteed debt, had been backed contractually by commodities as collateral?

Chapter Fifteen

Countertrade as a Way of Thinking

*"Too many U.S. companies still don't know
how to countertrade, even though they are
taking on offset commitments."*
—CARY VIKTOR, General Dynamics

REVIEWING COUNTERTRADE ISSUES

As Congress reviews the countertrade issue, it will be tempting to regulate U.S. companies, which are more accessible, rather than following the more difficult course of pressuring our allies to reduce their demands for military offset. The Senate is considering a bill (S-1892) to require the Secretaries of State and Defense to negotiate with our allies on the military offsets issue. The bill would also designate the Commerce Department as the lead agency to develop and administer a countertrade policy. I supported such a bill in testimony to the Senate Armed Services Committee. I would only caution that the Commerce Department focus must be on projecting U.S. offset policy overseas to our trading partners. U.S. companies need to offer creative packages if they are to win valuable sales, and it would not be in their interest if the bill were to regulate this practice through the Commerce Department or by any other means, short of multilateral agreements with U.S. trading partners.

Having served in government, I have seen a mismatch in the application of power between purpose and implementation. A distinction arises between where power *can* be applied, which is easier, and where it *should* be applied (on foreign governments requiring offsets), a much tougher course. Such a distinction may become relevant as the U.S. Congress debates current legislation and devotes more attention to the countertrade skills of U.S. corporations and to the status of countertrade and offset in the world.

It is tempting to view countertrade as simply an aberration of so-called free trade because it is somehow different from paying simple money for simple product. Taking this view, Congress could be tempted to pass laws restricting the ability of U.S. companies to use the valuable countertrade option. I believe such regulation would be the wrong focus and a mistake, making it more difficult for the larger U.S. companies to export at a time when our national need to export is greater than ever before.

FREE MARKET: BARTER AND OFFSET

Barter

In a way barter and offset are not anti-free market. They are free market. When it arises, barter is a problem-solver. It allows trade when currency problems in a country combine to work against trade. The ability of the purchaser to buy without convertible hard currency is but one advantage. The local sellers of barter products may also feel, as in the case of oil and other commodities, that they can get more value for their products than if they sold for cash. In some cases, commissions may be reduced or eliminated. In other cases, a faster turnaround time is possible, especially if the sellers' products would be hard to move for cash in a particularly competitive market niche. The advent of computerized trading worldwide could increase the secondary market for the consumer products and manufactured items that are priorities on national countertrade lists.

Offset

Offset is more complex. It has the aspect of extortion on a grand scale. The very idea that sensible countries like the United Kingdom, Switzerland, and Spain would request billions in offset sounds appalling. Yet, why shouldn't they? It facilitates their exports, brings in investment, builds co-production, and transfers technology to them.

At times I get irritated by the ease with which foreign governments impose an offset program successfully. In such moments I see offset as a kind of bribery on a massive scale where the sweetener is paid to a whole government, not an individual, and where the offset is in the best interests of large groups, an industrial sector, even the country itself. It is in the corporate nature of offset, where the recipients are large groups of people, that the analogy with bribery is out of place. Offset and the countertrade to support it are required by the officially mandated government policy of most of our major trading partners. Bribery, on the other hand, where a government individual is paid to influence a contract, is something that is prohibited by the Foreign Corrupt Practices Act.

However, there is no question that offset is a sweetener offered to a government by a seller in hopes of winning the sale. The offset is further driven by the intense nationalism and self-interest of the buying country. Because governments encourage offsets with such diligence and with so much leverage (created only in part by competitive pressures), at times their efforts do resemble extortion. Again, the large corporate and governmental dimensions of offset shatter this analogy. Offsets, carried out by governments on behalf of groups of people, are ultimately neither bribery nor extortion but good business in the hardball world of foreign trade.

The offset policies of U.S. trading partners work because intense competition for international contracts exists, not only among defense contractors and other companies in the United States, but among many companies in Europe, Canada, Australia, and Japan.

The offset policies of these trading partners may not be fair in the U.S. free-market sense, yet these policies are very effective because they are applied directly against a company, bypassing the United States government.

FINANCING ADVANTAGE

In a way, the countries requesting offset are also doing us a favor, giving us a way to compete where, surprise! Yankee ingenuity matters after all. Countertrade theoretically gives us a means to compete against the financing advantage of Europe and Japan and foreign companies generally. In the Rockwell–Zimbabwe printing press sale (see Chapter 7), countertrade overcame a French long-term 20-year credit of 4 percent. In the Rumanian turbine generator project (see Chapter 12), countertrade allowed the sale to survive even the collapse of a U.S. Export-Import Bank (Eximbank) financing offer. These transactions may be exceptional but they at least reveal one potential of countertrade, to offset a competitor's financing advantage in close bidding.

What is the financing advantage of Europe and Japan? Their governments have an almost fundamental, unchanging belief that government should finance larger manufactured exports (e.g., turnkey plants, heavy equipment, and power generating facilities) at longer terms and lower interest rates than available in the market, if such financing is necessary to win a sale. (The Japanese also have inherently lower market interest rates because their consumers save more money than consumers in the United States.) The major traditional vehicle in the United States to counter the trade financing advantages in Japan and Europe is the U.S. Eximbank. The Reagan Administration made it nearly impossible for Eximbank to finance large exports directly. This is a great irony for a supposedly business-oriented Administration and left many businesspeople, including the thousands who work for exporting companies, shaking their heads in disbelief.

If the financing advantage of the French or Japanese is 4 or 6 percent interest and that of the United States 10 or 11 percent interest, is it not theoretically hard to make up the difference with, say, 20 or 30 percent offset, let alone 100 percent? The Japanese could do the same, but are they really going to let countertraded products back into Japan? Would they let your friendly Yugoslavian foreign trade organization truck take hams to sell at their factory sites?

European offset requests also oblige the larger U.S. corporations to partner and cooperate with one another more than ever before. There are countless examples of cooperation between companies to get offset credit, through joint investment based on a subcontracting relationship or by attaching the procurement of foreign components to the credit of some other company's offset. A company such as Westinghouse forms a relationship to trade products by bringing in another, sometimes U.S., trading firm to take out countertraded products. In short, partnering and cooperation are important in competing well for international export sales. While European firms sometimes compete fiercely with one another, they also partner more naturally than U.S. counterparts for larger stakes such as the Airbus and various defense aerospace exports.

The Japanese companies struggle for market share at home but are more respectful of one another's territory overseas. I have heard of Japan's trading companies informally dividing up a foreign market such as Egypt into territories, where one trading company is dominant and others will not compete with it. Japanese companies, both trading and otherwise, are also famous for seeking joint-venture relationships with foreign companies.

One U.S. trading executive was understandably nervous about the ability of Japanese and European companies to cooperate relatively effectively. He observed that a major advantage of the U.S. Export Trading Company Act was to permit certain forms of collusion among trading companies.

In any event, he felt that more cooperation among U.S. companies is essential in countertrade. The formation in the past few years of the Defense Industries Offset Association and the nondefense-oriented American Countertrade Association is a helpful step in this direction.

HOPEFUL DEVELOPMENTS

In the sense of developing business style, the military offset requirements have also taken the already polished skills of a few leading U.S. corporations and raised them to a level approaching an art form. The countertrading skills of these companies have become a source of entrepreneurship and dealmaking in international trade that is refreshing and a hopeful development for our future competition with other world trading powers. Countertrading has helped open up new markets for the United States in Eastern Europe and difficult areas in the Third World. Offset has forced U.S. companies to set up new, profitable offices and subsidiaries in more traditional European markets and elsewhere, improving the parent company's prospects for new bidding there as with General Electric in Rumania, Douglas in Yugoslavia, and McDonnell-Douglas in Spain.

By requesting offset so vigorously, maybe the Europeans are on to something. The cost of developing military technologies has risen, especially after the oil price increases of the last decade. Even the most industrialized countries wanting to own state-of-the-art weapons find the cost burdensome. Countertrade in the sense of offset was invented partly to solve this problem. Its proponents in Europe have created several valid arguments. Jobs result from local content requirements. Lost foreign exchange is replaced by new export earnings, and potentially lost technology is nurtured by compensating and valuable subcontracts to the competing local industries that lose the bid. A few countries (e.g., Canada, Australia, and Switzerland) appear to have turned this philosophy of "breaking even" or "keeping pace" into a profitable national strategy by using it to build national industries that have a life of their own in the marketplace. The Japanese also appear determined to use offset for this purpose, to obtain technology transfer agreements. The Canadians made sure that when they signed the recent celebrated "free trade" agreement with the United States, their successful offset policies were untouched and left intact.

Perhaps it is time for the United States government to consider implementing its own offset policy, especially with countries where the U.S. trade deficit is severe and intractable (e.g., Japan, West Germany, and Taiwan). The attraction of such a policy is that it places the responsibility for the exporting not on a government whose power to persuade its companies to import more may be limited, but on the importing companies themselves. Following patterns already well established in the world, such a policy could also include more investment and co-production in the United States. A U.S. countertrade policy should emphasize the exporting of products from certain regions of the United States. This policy is carried out successfully in Canada.

As Europe and Japan become more successful in selling both low-tech and high-tech items to the Pentagon, there should be an insistence on tying these sales to exporting more from the United States. Barter could also be used on a government-to-government basis to get more value from American grain surpluses, rather than have grain rot in storage bins. Why not barter grain, at least surplus grain, for oil and strategic minerals or chemicals?

These policies are clearly interventionist (mostly counter-interventionist) but are more acceptable than protectionist barriers (e.g., increased quotas and retaliatory tariffs) because they foster response, mutuality, and integration. It is probably naïve for the United States to develop an offset policy merely as a bargaining chip to force Canada, Australia, and Europe to eliminate their offset policies. Most countries feel these policies are too successful to abandon. However, it may be possible through multilateral negotiations to put some downward pressure on the increasing percentages requested for offset by various countries.

DISADVANTAGES

The disadvantages to countertrade should not be overlooked. They can be serious. Companies are likely to put the cost of trading under an offset commitment into the price. The advantage a country gets by seeking exports through an offset can theoretically be less than the price increase in the initial sale to cover the cost of countertrading.

On a larger scale, many offset commitments in the world are still new and ongoing and have not come to full term. In other words, no one knows yet what will happen if a company fails to live up to these frequently large obligations. Will the contractual penalties be paid immediately or contested in long court battles? Will countries allege fraud and seek additional damages? Will a company with an unfulfilled commitment find future sales in that country impossible? While such contractual issues could create a whole new field for international lawyers and arbitrators, poorly negotiated and structured offset agreements are certainly bad business for companies.

In technology transfers under an offset there are two further issues, one concerning corporate strategy and the other national security. First, the company must evaluate how much the loss of technology will hurt it in future bids against a now technically enhanced competitor. General Dynamics (GD) is betting that F-16s from factories in the Netherlands or Turkey will not cut into sales. If they do, at least GD will earn some of the export proceeds, not to mention part of the proceeds from in-country sales. This is an advantage that co-production, based on equity ownership, has over a straight technology transfer. In other cases, a transfer has come back to haunt the seller. When Raytheon sold its Sparrow air-to-air missile to Italy, it agreed to transfer technology and equipment to a major Italian electronics company, Selenia Industrie Electtroniche Associate, and even to train Selenia technicians at a missile production facility in Lexington, Massachusetts. Now Selenia's missile, the Aspide, is sold as an Italian export and is cutting somewhat into the Sparrow's sales. Because development costs were low, the Aspide is cheaper than the Sparrow although some would debate Aspide's effectiveness.[7] The security issue is whether we are giving up too much costly technology too fast as a country, after having worked so hard to develop it. Will some of it end up in the wrong hands? Continued vigilance by the Commerce Department is very necessary as it reviews further technology transfer agreements, but balance and care are needed to avoid transfer reviews becoming overly restrictive.

In many instances barter and counterpurchase agreements have been used as last resorts for good reason. Such agreements may fail to materialize at a more technical level. Numerous problems must be solved, as illustrated by N-Ren International's barter transaction with Madagascar (see Chapter 8). There is the problem of agreeing on a formula for valuation and comparable value. An even greater problem is overcoming government regulations. Getting an approval in the right ministry can take months, although countries are now setting up specific bureaucracies to give clearer yes-or-no answers on proposed transactions. Many countries also provide no legal basis for buying export products with local currency. In Turkey, for example, barter is technically illegal, but would be permitted if a key ministry such as the defense ministry felt it was in the national interest.

A country may also face unresolved conflict with the International Monetary Fund (IMF). If arguments are pressed that allowing countertrade can generate incremental exports, create jobs, and help alleviate debt burden, IMF officials might become more supportive of the countertrade practice. In general, countertrade occurs in countries where the foreign exchange generated should, at least in theory, go to banks standing in line to collect on bad debts. Countries feel a few essentials are necessary and press ahead with barter and countertrade despite objections by the IMF and commercial banks seeking repayment of defaulted loans. For the country experiencing these difficulties, there appears to be no easy solution.

There are equally technical risks to companies seeking barter and counterpurchase. To avoid unwanted inventory, countertrade goods should be presold before taking title to them. But this is not always feasible. While some U.S. companies have taken the lead in creating countertrade units and even whole trading companies, many other companies are not organizing fast enough to conduct countertrade in the future. Cary Viktor made the dire observation that "too many U.S. companies still don't know how to counter-trade even though they are taking on offset commitments." The specialists who carry out offset and barter obligations must coordinate closely with the officers who negotiate the base sales agreements. The top managers of the companies need to be in touch with the specialists who live with and carry out the countertrade agreements and the company lawyers who have accumulated the experience of drafting them.

CONCLUSION

In the final analysis, there must be a willingness to walk away from a countertrade transaction when the numbers do not add up. Yet it also makes sense for U.S. companies to follow the lead of a General Electric or a General Dynamics by *thinking countertrade* in their business development and by becoming masters of the technique. These companies are finding new ways to make money from the opportunities presented. They are benefiting from the complexity and length of time, sometimes years, that it takes to complete one of these transactions. Because they understand the almost tribal importance of building the relationship and trust needed for the exchange to take place over time, they are successful. If there is an ultimate lesson for U.S. companies seeking to countertrade, it is to build up lasting relationships with countries.

Thinking countertrade also means extracting every ounce of export value from an import situation. This countertrade philosophy should ideally apply both to procurement officers of companies and to government officials.

The ability to think countertrade was illustrated beautifully by the Japanese during the recent proposed sale by RCA and its parent General Electric of the sophisticated electronic system aboard the *Aegis*, a major destroyer-type vessel in the U.S. Navy.

The Japanese government in 1988 insisted that the ships be built in Japan and that the electronic system be installed on a turnkey basis by RCA engineers sent to work in the

Japanese shipyard. U.S. critics argued that the Japanese should buy ships totally built in the United States. This would help the U.S. trade deficit even more and make it more difficult for Japanese engineers to learn about and copy the electronic system. Senator Johnston (D—La.) inserted language in the FY 1989 defense authorization bill requiring that the ships be built in the United States. Japan argued that it had not bought a foreign built ship in a hundred years and that it was paying RCA $500 million of the initial $1 billion cost for one destroyer anyway, with up to $200 million going to the Japanese shipbuilding company.

Japan stated the Johnston language would kill the sale. The Reagan Administration understandably wanted some sale rather than no sale, since the United States has argued for years that Japan should pay more for defense, or at least contribute more for foreign aid (as they are now doing). Secretary of State George Schultz and Secretary of Defense Frank Carlucci led an assault against the Johnston language with a joint op-ed column in *The Washington Post* (August 1, 1988). Senators Bradley (D—NJ) and Evans (R—Wash.) led a fight in the Senate that defeated the Johnston language by a margin of 75–20. However, U.S. anger about the trade deficit had surfaced on the Senate floor raising the prospect that protectionist tactics might be tried again if progress on the trade deficit does not continue.

The Japanese made a smart business decision and a good military one as well. The Reagan Administration was happy. RCA is pleased with a sale. While buying a major import, Japan made sure a sizable piece of the work, building the overall ship, was carried out in a Japanese shipyard. This minimized (or "offset") the outflow of yen from the country. The Japanese did not insist on a formal technology transfer agreement with RCA, as they have done for several other recent military purchases. No doubt, however, the defense electronics industry in Japan will benefit at least marginally from having RCA engineers, working next to Japanese engineers, installing the system in Japan. The day may not be far off when Japan joins the United States, the United Kingdom, France, and West Germany as a major exporter of defense equipment.

This incident illustrates the need for an overall framework of understanding between Japan and the United States on balancing trade. As the situation now stands, the United States has to chip away Japanese resistance to imports on a product basis, first beef, then oranges, then *Aegis* destroyers, and so on, causing a rift each time. As talks continue on a product basis, overall framework talks should proceed as well, giving the Japanese credit under an agreement for any exports from the United States, regardless of whether destined for Japan.

The RCA–Japanese transaction also shows how thinking countertrade, in the absence of a framework agreement, can be built around individual transactions, where every import represents a potential for loss that must somehow be offset or compensated.

Chapter Sixteen

Toward a National
Trade Policy

*"Could we finance for your U.S. client a sale against
commodities like we did in Jordan? Yes, I think so.
I'll get this cleared and call you back next week."*
—Mitsubishi Countertrade Specialist

The United States cannot make the rest of the world buy its products simply because it has the most powerful armed forces. While the military gives a certain ultimate credence to U.S. foreign policy, some other tools are necessary to give credibility to U.S. trade policy. An assortment of clever trade ideas with no way to be effective or implemented is not going to solve the U.S. trade deficit problem.

Two of the more effective tools are countertrade and government export credit financing. Thinking about countertrade helps to define some new approaches. The existence among the United States' major trading partners of offset policies for military and other high-tech systems demonstrates that the United States will not *begin* a trade war by developing some more aggressive policies of its own. The United States is already in the midst of a serious trade war, or certainly a fierce struggle, that it currently seems to be losing.

PURCHASING CLOUT

One of the key lessons taught by military offsets is that large national buyers have great clout. Their power to purchase large amounts of hardware in a competitive world gives them enormous leverage to make their policies effective, that is, to force sellers to comply with their offset policy or risk losing the business. Surely the United States as the largest consuming nation in the world can find a way to harness some of its purchasing power.

In developing a policy, perhaps asking for offsets should be considered when United States government purchases are made from overseas, in either the defense or nondefense areas. The United States should also insist that offset credit for government purchases overseas be awarded back to U.S.

companies, to help in fulfilling existing offset agreements that are being steadily added to with growing new offset demands from the countries buying their products.

A more difficult question has to do with determining whether any countertrade policies make sense in the private sector outside of the military area. The cheaper dollar has slowed but not drastically altered the flow of imports into the United States. Should the large exporter to the U.S. private sector (e.g., Mercedes Benz or Honda) be compelled through a countertrade policy to import more from the United States as a price of doing business? To address this question, some other issues must be considered.

U.S. export sales of more expensive items such as military equipment, commercial planes, and power plants are made to foreign governments or mostly state-owned corporations, whereas United States government purchases from foreign exporters are small compared with what our huge private sector buys from overseas. This helps to explain why we have been slow to develop countertrade policies in our own government, and why foreign governments have been quicker to impose offset requirements. These requests have arisen fastest in countries where major government purchasing takes place, e.g., in Europe, Japan, and the Third World.

Beyond the issue of where our purchasing clout lies, we also have another disadvantage, a relatively low need for technology transfer. Foreign countries use countertrade for what they need or want, and technology transfer is high on the list. Japan hardly needs countertrade to generate Japanese exports, but the government has used it to compel technology transfer from U.S. defense contractors in several notable cases. The most recent of these involves General Dynamics' (GD) sale of an F-16 to Japan called the FSX. The Japanese accomplished some interesting trade objectives in this purchase. It appears they are making a major import from the United States, placating Congress and the White House. Yet they selected the F-16 in part because it, among the competing U.S. planes, can be most easily modified, allowing it to be crammed with Japanese components and electronics. Mitsubishi will jointly develop the plane under license with GD. Assuring that much of the technology will be transferred to Japan while allowing so much Japanese content, there probably will not be much impact on the trade balance. Mitsubishi wanted to develop the plane on its own, and used this alleged capability as a bargaining tactic.

Back to the question we asked earlier, should a large exporter to the United States be compelled to import more from the United States as a price of doing business? If the falling dollar does not slow imports sufficiently, if the threat of retaliatory tariffs does not open up closed foreign market sectors for us, well, something has to give somewhere. Countertrade can be used to crack barriers and open markets, as understood very clearly by the Swiss military attaché described in Chapter 4 and by European governments generally. The concept of requiring foreign companies to match selected additional exports into the United States with imports from the United States is one that should be examined carefully. Japanese trading companies, like C. Itoh and Mitsubishi, with their large trading networks, are already well suited to adapt to this policy. They already import significantly *from* the United States, to Japan and elsewhere, and with the right prodding and incentives could be persuaded to make even more purchases of U.S. products.

One of the peculiarities of the trade struggle now being waged in the world is that trade, unlike defense, allows everyone to "hit and talk" at the same time, so that negotiations should no doubt accompany whatever new measures we enact.

There are other countertrade tools that ought to be looked at, like U.S.-sponsored barter of surplus wheat it owns or may want to buy, for oil and strategic minerals and chemicals.

NEED FOR U.S. TRADING COMPANY

It is time for the United States to consider establishing or buying its own government trading company, formalizing some buying and selling functions already fulfilled by the Department of Agriculture. Would such a trading company give us more flexibility to trade commodities in parts of the world (i.e., much of the world) where blocked currencies and scarce foreign exchange are making trade difficult? Could we not advance some U.S. national security interests in Latin America, Africa, India, Pakistan, or Eastern Europe with such a company?

In a world where military offsets and blocked currencies necessitate both military and commercial countertrade, U.S. interests are still impaired by the lack of at least one strong general trading company located in the United States! Some of our grain trading companies and Phibro in New York are moving into countertrade as a service business for U.S. clients, but not yet nearly so effectively as Mitsubishi, for example, which has assisted not only Japanese but U.S. bids, as in the Westinghouse–Jordan transaction. Japanese trading companies, and on a smaller scale their West German counterparts, give their nations' manufacturing firms an advantage when countertrade is required to make a sale.

Americans who work outside the international business area would be surprised at how often major U.S. manufacturing companies in areas such as defense, telecommunications, or commerical aircraft must rely on foreign trading companies, especially Japanese, to service their growing countertrade requirements.

If a United States government-sponsored trading company grew and became successful, it could certainly be sold to the private sector. There is a precedent for a publicly owned company performing at least one government mission with some government control. Communications Satellite Corporation (COMSAT) is a publicly traded company with significant United States government membership on its board and is also the U.S. signatory of the Intellsat agreement concerning overseas phone traffic via satellite.

GOVERNMENT EXPORT CREDIT

Another major tool in a national trade policy must surely be in the area of government financing. If countertrade arouses some controversy, the idea of government financing arouses real passions.

Part of the problem is rhetorical. Export-Import Bank's (Eximbank) budget is considered each year by Congress in the same category—"150," foreign aid—and thus must compete with the State Department's AID (the Agency for International Development) for budget authority. For this and other reasons, Eximbank's lending and budget are sometimes wrongly considered foreign aid in the sense of a "giveaway" program or grant more typical of AID funding. Under the new spending restraints imposed by the Gramm-Rudman-Hollings Act, foreign aid will increasingly be subjected to budget cutting pressure. Even without Gramm-Rudman, foreign aid has always been an easy target for politicians to rail against. A frequent complaint by constituents is, "We need domestic aid, not foreign aid."

I believe it would be beneficial to U.S. exporters to pull Eximbank out of the foreign aid ("150") category and put it elsewhere in the Federal budget.

If the truth be known, Eximbank's export credits *are* "domestic aid" of the best sort! First, these credits help U.S. companies grow in the United States by developing export markets through competitive financing. There is no stimulus for exports like competitive financing. Foreign borrowers of Eximbank loans would get similar terms anyway from Eximbank's competitors in Europe and Japan, so why not bring this business to our domestic manufacturers of export products. Second, the money lent is usually repaid by the foreign borrowers. Eximbank credits are neither grants to the foreign borrower nor grants to the domestic producer. Eximbank credit is a domestic aid program that is *not* a "giveaway" program. Third, the availability of Eximbank credit provides incentives for U.S. manufacturers not to source business overseas simply to get attractive financing. A fourth point should not be forgotten. Once a trade policy begins to work, and our trade deficit improves, the U.S. dollar will get stronger, making our exports once again more expensive. In these conditions, government financing will be even more critical, and we will need Eximbank to be in an especially sharpened state of readiness. The strong dollar coupled with a sharply reduced Eximbank budget in the early 1980s was an especially deadly combination for U.S. exporters of larger manufactured products. Attractive financing is needed to compensate for the effects of a strong currency. Japanese companies have found this to be true now with their strong yen. They have responded by accepting lower profits, and by emphasizing financing skills, ranging from countertrade expertise in places like the People's Republic of China to government export credit. Japanese trade policy and corporations have understood how difficult it is to regain market share once it is lost. A vice president at Eximbank confirmed that while all of its competitors saw their business decline in the economic slowdown of the early 1980s, they all continued to market their financing programs aggressively.

I believe it is in the best interests of the United States for Eximbank to sharply increase its direct lending programs.

A natural concern must be, if Eximbank were to seriously increase its lending, would it experience massive defaults as happened with commercial banks in areas such as Latin America and Iran? In the past, Eximbank's record for receiving repayment has been excellent. For Iran, Eximbank negotiated a settlement against the Iranian assets frozen outside the country. More than 90 percent of this portfolio was repaid. In Latin America, Eximbank has been effective in getting repaid by the Brazilian and Mexican governments. The Brazilians are repaying their rescheduled debt to Eximbank and are negotiating actively to reschedule some additional loans. Mexico is current on repayment of all its rescheduled public debt. Out of $470 million paid by Eximbank on claims against Mexican private sector debt, Eximbank has collected already $180 million in cash and expects substantial additional recovery. Steve Proctor, who leads Eximbank's Claims and Recovery Division, and his deputies, Peter Vatter and George Henderson, were presented a special award by Treasury Secretary James Baker for this remarkable collection effort.

Eximbank almost never writes off government-secured debt and has little need to because of its repayment successes. Countries repay their government-backed debt to Eximbank because they want to borrow new money. Two rare examples of uncollected Eximbank public debt help to demonstrate how unusual the occurrence is and how hard the bank tries to collect. In the late 1970s, the People's

Republic of China disavowed loans made in the 1940s to its revolutionary opponent, the Kuomintang government. Eximbank pursued collection on these loans for 30 years and abandoned the quest only when told to do so by higher government authorities. A legendary attempt to collect repayment on loans to the pre-Castro government of Cuba was made by Walter Sauer in the 1960s. Sauer, who was an acting chairman of Eximbank and worked there from 1935 to 1980, personally visited Cuba at some personal risk to himself. Castro delayed for several days hoping Sauer would just leave. Then he scheduled a midnight meeting, hoping to discourage the persistent United States government banker. Sauer showed up anyway, forcing Castro to tell him face-to-face he would not repay. To this day, the bank has written off less than 1 percent of its multibillion-dollar portfolio, at least in the area of government-secured debt.

Commercial bankers, like U.S. exporters, view Eximbank as a stimulus to their own banking business as well. There is usually room for commercial credit in an Eximbank loan package. The commercial bankers, aware of Eximbank's excellent repayment record, feel a measure of additional security when Eximbank is co-lender on a project, even when not a guarantor of the commercial bank portion of the package.

Eximbank is, in short, a misunderstood, little-known, and hidden jewel in the United States government with the potential to play a major role in a United States government-sponsored trade rejuvenation program. One of the easiest ways to increase Eximbank's budget in an era of budget restraint is simply to take it out of the budget, as was done for 1971–1976. Since loans are always being repaid, only shortfalls on a cash flow basis ought to impact the overall U.S. budget. These shortfalls have been minuscule compared to the Eximbank budget authorization figure each year.

Indeed, as already pointed out, Eximbank during much of its history, even when lending actively, made a profit. Only Eximbank's actual subsidy should be included in the Federal budget. If it can make a profit in a given year, then it should have no impact. The Credit Reform Act, proposed in 1987 but not enacted, actually calls for this approach. I hope this idea will see the light of day.

Eximbank can make a profit and have a major impact on our trade deficit at the same time. Most governments of the developed world think the export credit approach is invaluable even when it loses some money.

Thought should also be given to replacing some of AID's grant programs currently being cut back with very low interest loans spread over long terms, with only the actual subsidy element being counted in the budget. The same approach could also be used for Foreign Military Sales (FMS) grants and some credits from the Pentagon, also under the budget cutting process. These programs benefit U.S. exporters too. The Japanese and French have proven to be masters of mixing extremely low interest "aid" credit with export credit and commercial bank loans to promote their domestic exporters.

Also, most foreign export credit agencies can finance military sales, whereas Eximbank is still prohibited from such an activity for its Third World market. This should be changed, especially if FMS credits must be curtailed as part of Pentagon budget cutting. Eximbank could play an important role here, in helping to finance U.S. military sales overseas where competitive financing is key to making the export.

The United States must stop the current situation where its exporters (whether oriented toward defense or toward commercial sectors) go into an overseas bid knowing their financing package is going to be beaten by foreign export credit. The only way to deal with this problem is to compete with excellent U.S. financing instruments.

In a discussion about trade issues, one State Department official made an ironic observation about the rising influx of Japanese and European investment in the United States: "The only thing worse than having the Japanese buy up large segments of American industry and real estate is if they did *not* invest in this country." He meant that Japanese investment in the United States works to reduce the U.S. trade deficit and in that sense is a substitute for reduced ability to sell products to Japan. I would rather sell products to Japan and reduce the trade deficit that way.

Taken together, countertrade and export credit create reasons to trade with U.S. companies based on reciprocity and truly competitive financing. This is a proactive and promotional approach to the exporting part of the trade deficit equation. As the United States moves in this direction, I hope its trading partners will be responsive, encouraging U.S. exports while reducing their barriers, quotas, and tariffs. After all, the United States is a net buyer to some of these trading partners. If U.S. financing instruments and a countertrade policy are not allowed to work, this buyer may turn in frustration once more to protectionist measures.

COHERENT POLICY

If foreign trade policy were taken as seriously as national security policy, U.S. companies would benefit greatly. U.S. trade policy is hurt by both the lack of strong players and the fragmentation of too many disparate players. The State Department, Pentagon, Commerce, Agriculture, and Treasury Departments, the Office of Management and Budget, the Special Trade Representatives' Office, and several other government agencies play a role in trade. The Commerce Department has had a sad history of losing many battles on trade policy to these other agencies when it should be playing the lead role.

It needs tools to do this, such as the exclusive responsibility to administrate a U.S. countertrade or offset policy and to advise Eximbank and other government finance agencies on export loans. Congress has talked about strengthening the Commerce Department for years but no progress will ever be realized unless Commerce is given tools beyond the granting of export licenses, its current principal function. Select, additional recruiting across government agencies and from talent outside government will be needed for the Commerce Department if its responsibilities are expanded by Congress.

Strong leadership by one central trade agency is important because coherence is needed to maximize exports. Many policies and instruments must work toward this one, all-important goal. Someone has to be sure that new tax laws have favorable and not unfavorable consequences for U.S. exporters. Someone has to coordinate political pressure when it is needed to enhance our export sales. Someone has to argue that a better financing package, from somewhere in the United States government, is critical to a U.S. company's chances of winning a sale. Someone will have to coordinate trade negotiations to reduce offsets, with the implementation of our own offset policy. Perhaps a U.S. trading company could enhance and complement a greatly strengthened Commerce Department. U.S. trade policy needs better tools and more coherence if it is to project the exports and influence of U.S. companies into the world.

References

1. Gabriel Wujek, "Polish Perception of Countertrade," in *Countertrade: International Trade Without Cash*. Chairman: Peter D. Ehrenhaft (New York: Law and Business, Inc., Harcourt, Brace, Jovanovich, 1984), pp. 240–246.
2. Office of Management and Budget (OMB), "Impact of Offsets in Defense-Related Exports," paper prepared by OMB, December 1985.
3. Eileen White, *The Wall Street Journal*, September 10, 1987, pp. 1 and 15.
4. Hobart Rowan, *The Washington Post*, January 27, 1988, Section 7, pp. 1 and 5.
5. *Euromoney Trade Finance Report*, December 1986, p. 41.
6. Clay Chandler, *The Washington Post*, July 14, 1987, p. E3.
7. Clyde H. Farnsworth, *International Herald Tribune*, December 9, 1986, pp. 1 and 15.
8. John W. Dizzard, "The Explosion of International Barter," *Fortune Magazine*, February 7, 1983 (reprinted in Ref. 2, p. 19).
9. T. A. Campobasso, "The Third World and Countertrade," in *Countertrade: International Trade Without Cash*, Chairman: Peter D. Ehrenhaft (New York: Law and Business Inc., Harcourt, Brace, Jovanovich, 1984), pp. 27–29.
10. Donald Southerland, *The Washington Post*, August 1, 1987, p. D1.

References

11. Jim Barkus, "A Bank's Role in Facilitating and Financing Counter-trade," in *International Countertrade*. Editor: Christopher Korth (New York and London: Quorum Books, 1987), p. 79.

12. Pompiliu Verzariu, *Countertrade Practices in Eastern Europe, the Soviet Union and China* (Washington, DC: U.S. Department of Commerce, 1980), pp. 78 and 79.

13. Marcel Mauss, *The Gift: Forms and Functions of Exchange in Archaic Societies* (London: Cohen & West Ltd., 1969).

14. Claude Levi-Strauss, *The Elementary Structures of Kinship*. Translated by J. H. Hall, J. R. Von Sturmer, and Rodney Needham (London: Eyre & Spottiswoode, 1969. First published in France in 1949), pp. 62–65.

15. R. H. Barnes, *Kedang: A Study of the Collective Thought of an Eastern Indonesian People* (Oxford: Clarendon Press, 1974), pp. 228–289.

16. Matt Schaffer and Christine Cooper, *Mandinko: The Ethnography of a West African Holy Land* (Prospect Heights, Ill.: The Waveland Press, 1987 and New York: Holt, Rinehart and Winston, 1980), pp. 80 and 81.

17. Napoleon Chagnon, *Yanomano: The Fierce People* (New York: Holt, Rinehart and Winston, 1968), pp. 100 and 101.

Name
Index

Name Index

Eastern Bloc, 93, 124, 140–144, 146–154
Eastern Europe, 6, 24, 135–137, 191, 203
Eaton Corporation, 148
ECGD, 26, 88
Ecuador, 85, 107
EEC, 177
Egypt, 89, 91, 93, 94
Enterprise Electronics, 75
Ericsson, 110
Europe, 10, 28, 65, 188, 189, 193, 201, 205
Evans, Senator (R—Wash.), 197
Eximbank, 21, 22–24, 25, 29–31, 88, 110–111, 136, 152, 189, 204–209, 206, 210
Eximbank of Japan, 25, 119
Exocet missiles, 83
Export Trading Company Act, 111, 180, 190

F-5, 51–53, 72
F-15, 118
F-16, 2, 9, 16, 19, 31, 38–45, 64, 118, 164, 170, 194, 201
F-18, 60, 73, 74, 75
Federal Financing Bank (FFB), 25, 26
Ferranti Co., 57
Ferrostaal Co., 98
Finland, 153
Finley, Emil, 122
First Boston, 111, 180
Ford Aerospace, 75
Ford, Gerald, 30
Foreign Corrupt Practices Act, 188
Foreign Military Sales (FMS) credits, 22, 26, 27, 29, 32–33, 39, 49, 50, 119, 164, 173
Foreign aid category "150," 204–205
France, 16, 17, 23, 26, 28, 41, 58, 82, 86, 93, 145, 170, 176
Frankfurt, 148
FSX, 118
Fuji Bank, 34

Gabon, 88, 171

Gambia, 158
Gaz de France, 86
Geacamines, 92
GE Trading Company, 152, 168, 171–172
General Agreement on Tariffs and Trade (GATT), 10, 11, 69, 177
General Dynamics, 2, 9, 16, 19, 31, 37, 38–40, 50, 64, 118, 164, 168–171, 176, 194, 196, 201, 202
General Electric, 2, 39–41, 52, 62, 72, 152, 181, 191, 196–198
General Electric of the U.K., 57
General Motors, 148, 178–179, 181
Geneva, 180
Genex, 136
Georgetown University, 11
Germany, 6
Ghana, 92
Golan-nor Company, 145
Gramm-Rudman-Hollings Act, 204
Greece, 38, 43, 64, 171
Green Island Cement, 120
Grumman, 119
Guilfoil, Petzall and Shoemake, 95
Guinea, 92

Hall, Pat, 88–89, 169, 180
Hamburg, 32, 99, 101, 102
Hamilton, Francis, 110
Hamilton Brothers Oil, 85
Harpoon missile, 118
Harris, 87
Hart, Don, 95, 99, 102, 104
Harvard Business School, 152
Helene Curtis, 123
Hellenic Business Development and Investment Company, 170
Henderson, George, 206
Hercules, 119
Hermes, 25, 27, 31–33
Honda, 201
Hong Kong, 120, 137, 180
Hughes Aircraft, 53–54
Hull, Cordell, 97

Name Index

Name Index

Viktor, Cary, 37, 38, 42, 43, 44, 180, 195
Vodka, 145
Voest Alpine Co., 97–98
Volkswagen, 83
Volvo, 82–83, 85

Wall Street Journal, 9, 62
Washington Post, 197
Washington, D.C., 12, 14, 135, 144
West Germany, 10, 11, 21, 27, 28, 43, 57–58, 142–144, 145, 192, 198
West, Dan, 179
Western Europe, 142–144

Westinghouse, 39–41, 63, 75, 80, 117, 135, 146, 170, 172–174, 178, 181, 190
White, Eileen, 117
White House, 10, 15, 202
Wraxall Group, 173
Wujek, Gabriel, 147

Yanomamo, 163
Yugoslavia, 4, 6, 20, 29, 130–137, 177, 191

Zaire, 88, 92
Zambia, 90
Zimbabwe, 2, 26, 88–90

Subject
Index